PRA

MAKING A CASE FOR INNOCENCE

"Through a series of case studies, written more in the style of short stories than the sleep-inducing, dry academic speak of typical post-case-analysis reports, Higuera takes the reader into the grit and grime of murder and mayhem. I started this book early in the morning and had eagerly consumed every page by early evening. April Higuera shares wit and humor and hard-won knowledge. To the curious, the newly minted, and the hard-boiled detective I say: Go buy this book."

– **Hal Humphreys**, Executive Editor of *Pursuit Magazine*

"April takes you on a backdoor ride of the unsung hero as the investigator who deserves the credit for solving crimes and releasing criminally charged innocent men. This book serves all folks involved in the criminal justice system."

– **Mary Lou Wilson, Esq.**, Post-Conviction Attorney

"I love this book! Makes me wish I was more than just a Legal Secretary so I could support the cause."

– **Julie C.**, a Public Defender's Office secretary

"Evocative personal and professional memoirs of a criminal defense investigator. Excellent writing and points on the justice system. A VERY GOOD READ!"

– **former prosecutor** (who prefers to remain anonymous)

"April provides riveting and provocative sights in the world of defense investigation. Her passion and commitment for the truth is evident on each page. Real-life stories are told in factual accounts interjected with honesty and humor. This book demonstrates how a knowledgeable defense investigator can tip the scales of justice. A must-read for all; especially those oblivious to the inequities in the judicial system."

— **Lori N.,** corporate accounting professional

"THANK YOU Ms. Higuera for writing 'Making A Case For Innocence.' I wish I had millions of dollars to buy and send it to every police officer, prosecutor and judge in this country! Every one of them, and attorneys as well, NEED to read it!"

— **Fran H.**, mother fighting to overturn her son's wrongful conviction

"I came away from this book truly admiring the fearlessness of the author, April Higuera. Hired to assist a legal team as a 'newbie' defense investigator, she is soon digging up clues on major murder cases that in some cases point to actual innocence. Her strong sense of Justice-with-a-capital-J (as opposed to mere lock-em-up 'law and order') propels her to pursue evidence that others have overlooked — or purposely obscured."

— **Alexandra T.**, music professional

TRUE STORIES OF A CRIMINAL DEFENSE INVESTIGATOR

APRIL HIGUERA

PUBLISHED BY APRIL HIGUERA • RENO, NV

All rights reserved.
© Copyright 2016 by April D. Higuera
ISBN: 978-0-9979943-0-8

No part of this book may be reproduced or transmitted in any form or by any means, electronic or mechanical, including photocopying, recording,or by any information storage or retrieval system, without permission in writing from the publisher.

Copyright Notice
Published by April Higuera
316 California Av #50, Reno, NV 89509

LEGAL NOTICE: While all attempts have been made to verify information provided in this publication, the author/publisher assumes no responsibility for errors, omissions, or contradictory interpretation of the subject matter herein. The purchaser or reader of this publication assumes responsibility for the use of these materials, information, and for adherence to all the applicable laws and regulations governing professional licensing, business practices, advertising, and any other aspects of doing business in the purchaser's or reader's respective jurisdiction of residence or business. The author/publisher assumes no responsibility or liability whatsoever on behalf of any purchaser or reader of these materials. Any perceived slights of specific people or organizations are not intended to harm any person or organization, but only to inform based on the actual experiences of and/or readings by the author. The purchaser/reader acknowledges that the content provided in this book is for informational purposes only and that risk of business failure is based on the strategies and plans devised and executed by the purchaser's/reader's themselves. The purchaser/reader thus agrees that the author/publisher is not responsible for successes or failures of purchaser's/reader's personal and business decisions relating to this any information provided in this book. My mentions of "alternate suspects" is not intended to formally accuse such persons of any wrongdoing. These persons have not been investigated by law enforcement nor officially accused of any criminal or unethical activity, but merely people that my investigation uncovered as potentially having motive and opportunity. Do not assume any guilt based upon my inferences and investigation. My use of photos of defendants is by permission from the defendant's family and/or the defendants themselves. Any reproduction of any photos in this book, without express written permission, is strictly prohibited.

Dedication

Justice is about the truth.
In the criminal justice system, we come from both sides to find the truth without ever taking sides. This book is dedicated to the honest men and women working in the justice system and to all the innocent citizens wrongly accused of crimes and their families.

I especially thank Sedley Alley's and Max Roybal's daughters, who were courageous enough to contribute to this book through conversations with me about their fathers' incarcerations and legal battles.

Acknowledgements

I sincerely thank my family, my good friends, and my colleagues for their support and contributions to this book. Much of the review, photography, graphics, design, and editing was achieved through the efforts of these great and trusted companions. I so appreciate all of the love and time spent, and I am so happy to share this work we have created together.

Special thanks to Alex Forbes (editor, back cover, and book interior designer), Quintin Chatman (editor), Sarah-Jane Higuera (editor), Tommy O'Brien (cover photographer and front cover designer), Jorey Krawczyn (foreword author), Audrey Reille (success coach), and those friends and family that reviewed my manuscript as the book developed.

Special thanks also to "Anne" for allowing me to share our personal stories, for her insightful and passionate thirst for the truth, and her invaluable assistance in my investigation casework at the beginning of my career.

Extra special thanks, once again to all of Sedley Alley's and Max Roybal's children, who granted permissions and participated in the writing of their fathers' stories, and to Hope Schreiner and Jamal Shakir for allowing me to write about their cases in detail.

Table of Contents

Foreword
By Dr. Jorey Krawczyn

By definition, systems impact and are impacted by each other. This book focuses on the defense functions as they work with the other major components of the criminal justice system – courts and law enforcement.

Varying definitions and perspectives on criminality impact the practice of law and the idea of justice across time and society. In turn, the police, courts, and defense elements of the system are affected as all three strive to work together toward a common goal called "justice." As the author postulates, even the definition of the term justice is often contextual.

Over the past 50 years the criminal justice system has suffered many changes as it continues to address the social problem of criminal behaviors. There are currently two models being followed: the Crime Control Model, which focuses primarily on rights of society to be protected from crime and criminals, and the Due Process Model, which places primary focus on the rights of individual to be protected from government powers.

These are sound theoretical concepts. However, in application the results have been a system driven by police arrests and prosecutor convictions, while justice takes a back seat. There can be very little justice in the current criminal justice system.

This book demonstrates the need to regain judicial clarity, and the significant role that is played by an ethical judicial investigator, i.e. one who works for justice, and not for the police or prosecution.

At one time in the history of the criminal justice system, police filled that role as purveyors of truth and justice. Arrest and conviction rates have greatly altered that role, and the standard of justice has suffered—as well as the innocent who have been convicted and even executed.

The book eloquently explores the criminal justice system's use of the forensic analysis of police science while correlating the fallacies through the case examples. The system serves as its own peer review committee, and with each conviction police science is further validated. As a judge once explained, "Police science has done for science, what marching bands have done for music."

A glaring factor which is an undertone throughout this book, and which is seldom discussed within the criminal justice system, is the dynamic of justice denied to all victims of the system's dysfunctionality. A systems model that has been gaining influence throughout the world seeks to make the victims whole.

It is called Restorative Justice, and it currently holds to the concept of restoring the crime victims to their original state of being via the criminal justice system. If the court issues a ruling of not guilty in part due to the dedicated work of a defense investigator, there still remains a crime committed and a guilty party somewhere waiting to be brought to justice. Seldom do we hear of police and prosecution re-opening a case to locate the true guilty party. The system professionally moves on to the next arrest and conviction.

This book constantly reiterates the conceptualization of truth and justice. Is one subservient while the other is superior, or are they equal partners in an adversarial system? At the end of the systematic process do they balance the scales of justice? The book shows that a well-trained, ethical defense investigator can be the variable within the systematic process to impact the scales of justice and bring about a balance.

– Jorey Krawczyn

July 2016

CREDENTIALS: Dr. Jorey Krawczyn is currently working within the U.S. Department of State, Bureau of International Narcotics and Law Enforcement Affairs, and is an instructor in the International Law Enforcement Academy.

INTRODUCTION

No system can achieve perfect justice, in my opinion, if humans make the decisions. This book speaks to this sad reality. The crux of my exposés, the main purpose of my writing this book, and where my heart lives while investigating cases on behalf of the defense, is to bring balance to an off-kilter criminal justice system.

You might be surprised to learn that I am not a crusader, nor a bleeding heart liberal, and I am not in the business of setting criminals free. My purpose is to protect all citizens from human error and greed within our justice system. Guilty people go to jail. Innocent people should not.

This book is about uncovering innocence; how every criminal case should be zealously investigated on behalf of the defendant, even if he or she confessed.

This book is about prosecutorial corruption and honest error, and how competent defense investigation and advocacy result in the justice system working as intended. I value and applaud good and just law enforcement officers, prosecutors, judges, jurors, and defense professionals. I call out corrupt ones.

The National Registry of Exonerations information indicates that 149 people were exonerated in the United States and its territories last year alone (2015). [1]

It was further reported through the Registry that those exonerated served an average of 14.5 years of incarceration. These people were convicted while innocent! How does this happen? Why are wrongful convictions so prevalent? Where does the system go wrong?

Jurors are typically inexperienced in the law. Most often, they have never been through the criminal justice system, and are naively ignorant of the prevalence of official misconduct by police officers and prosecutors that pervades our far too often "unjust" legal system.

Simply said, once you are in handcuffs, the cards are stacked against you. Only a defense team can rescue you after arrest. And if you can't afford a good defense team, God help you!

I recently spoke "off the record" with an ex-prosecutor who, while supporting the content of this book, explained that prosecutors are often overwhelmed with cases and rely upon the information presented to them by the police. She confided to me that she has tried up to seven cases in one day! Seven actual trials. Overloaded and underfunded.

The same issue arises for public defenders.

Some prosecutors truly believe they are doing God's work . . . fighting the good fight for a lesser salary, while some private defense attorneys are making millions.

This ex-prosecutor's point is that prosecution oversights (errors concerning true facts of a case) are inadvertent because government attorneys rely heavily on the police to provide the facts of a case. I asked her why a prosecutor might lie to get a conviction. She didn't have an answer because, in her individual experience, she is not aware of any such intentional betrayals of justice. Instead, she responded, "At the end of the day, we want justice." I applaud her personal integrity, however, we all know that not all criminal justice professionals hone the sword of truth.

With regard to relying upon the police to provide accurate facts surrounding an allegation, I recently read an editorial by a black ex-cop named Redditt Hudson who concluded that, in his experience on the police force, 15 percent of the cops are always honest, 15 percent of the cops are corrupt, and the remaining 70 percent can go either way depending upon the supervisor's requests. [2]

These percentages are pretty scary, but I'm not sure they are wrong. In all fairness, there is an article written as commentary on Hudson's article which calls out Hudson as a "wannabe politician" and which states that his numbers are wrong. [3]

In the last two trials for cases in which I investigated for defense, a cop literally lied, in my opinion, on the stand (one merely stated that he changed his opinion). Why??? I'm thinking that the cops truly believed they arrested the right guy and wanted to put him away, no matter what. My argument is, however, that the facts should speak for themselves. When I testify, I do not lie . . . ever. Why would I be so arrogant as to assume I know everything. I'm just testifying about what I experienced, and that's all a cop should ever do as well.

In my 15 years as a criminal defense investigator, I have run into several corrupt officers, others who were merely incompetent, or like the ex-prosecutor said, good cops overloaded with cases. Lack of funding is a huge problem in our country. Seven trials in one day, by an individual prosecutor, is insanity. We need more cops, more public defenders, and more prosecutors to help ensure that each case gets the attention it deserves.

Not only are citizens getting the sharp end of the stick with wrongful arrests and convictions, but the rest of us are paying for it. The city of Chicago reportedly paid out $500 million in settlements for police misconduct over the decade prior to 2014. In 2011, Los Angeles paid out $54 million and New York paid out $735 million. And other cities like Dallas, Oakland, and Minneapolis paid out huge sums as well . . . settling cases with citizens who were victims of police misconduct and abuse. [4]

This book brings you deep inside the typically confidential aspects of several criminal cases as I take you along with me on my journey as a defense investigator. The public rarely hears about this undercover journey.

From presumed guilt to factual innocence, I attempt to explain the legal system in common, everyday terms and reveal the process of my investigation in several media-driven and high profile homicide cases. Along the way, I describe my inner journey from non-believer to believer that the system is broken and that defense teams can be heroes.

I share my inner thoughts with you: how these cases contributed to my personal growth, and my shift from a life focused on a dream of fame and fortune in the music industry to the dream of a justice system that is truth-based and fair in protecting all citizens.

I begin this book lightly with two stories of my personal experiences within my casework, and later delve into the dark and intimate investigative footwork and the details of actual cases. As expected, I offer commentary, but I am going to leave the answers up to you.

Through my work experiences, I moved from a personal position I could describe as unsympathetic and fearful to a place of understanding and compassion. Moreover, through my defense investigation experiences, my eyes have opened to the ineffectiveness of the justice system and to the realization that it does not always function as intended.

I have come full circle in awakening to the fact that defense attorneys and investigators are, unfortunately, necessary.

It might come as a shock to some of you how carelessly, or intentionally, the truth is sometimes left to drown beneath the muddy waters of criminal justice. Turning these pages and absorbing the gripping true events of average citizens facing life in prison—and worse—is likely to instill an intense range of emotions. Hopefully it will also raise awareness of the flaws in the criminal justice system as you delve into the actual investigations, uncovering additional evidence, and unwinding criminal cases with me.

The important role of competent defense in keeping all of us safe from the unfortunate prevalence of malicious prosecution cannot be overestimated. For anyone who has been sleeping, this is a wake-up call.

– April Higuera
July 2016

DISCLAIMER: While the events in these stories are TRUE, and are described accurately to the best of my recollection, I have changed the names of all witnesses and alternate suspects, and I have altered minor details of actual conversations and events in order to protect the privacy of persons and offer the gist of actual conversations and activities without verbatim transcription. Please excuse any inadvertent errors in my recollection. If I have left anything out it might be because that specific information remains confidential in nature. My use of lower case letters for "black" and "white" people is in no way intended to be disrespectful, but only representative of my understanding of current writing style trends. My sincere apologies if such is offensive to anyone. Additionally, mentioning authors and legal professionals by name or inference is never meant to individually criticize, but only to emphasize my perceptions based on my personal experiences.

Jamal Shakir: Colors

Clear blue sky over my head, dirty gray cement below my feet, and smoky black soot from burnt gunpowder invading my nostrils. This is Compton, California, gangland USA, home of the infamous and violent black gangs, the Crips and Bloods.

This is my first trip to this area of our country. I am green, a newbie. The car rental agency handed me keys to a bright red Toyota compact. I drove to this address to meet defense attorney Natman Schaye, and work on the Jamal Shakir homicide case—a case in which the federal government is seeking a death sentence.

Here I stand with Natman on the hot pavement in front of Jamal's family home. We are clearly the only white people as far as the eyes can see. He is wearing a crisp beige western hat, turquoise bolo tie, and brown snakeskin cowboy boots. I suppose this is customary attire for criminal defense attorneys from Tucson, Arizona. He is an expert in his field, defending persons facing capital murder charges, with the broader mission to abolish the death penalty.

Me? I'm a part-time paralegal at a Nashville, Tennessee, law firm just out of college, paying the bills as I continue to work on my childhood dream of becoming a famous singer/songwriter. Not too long ago, I was center-stage as a female vocalist on the national TV show *Star Search* hosted by Ed McMahon (the *American Idol* of old). It's a far cry from this drug-infested war zone.

I'm only standing on this corner today because the federal government is withholding funds from the Shakir defense team, which includes an attorney from the law firm where I work. This means the defense team cannot hire a private investigator to help on Jamal's behalf. So, tag, I'm it!

I volunteered. I like challenges and new adventures. I have zero training.

My main task in this case is to digest over 30,000 pages of law enforcement investigation, though now my involvement has been extended to assist attorney Schaye at trial on a kidnapping with deadly weapon charge for Mr. Shakir in a Los Angeles court.

I never had any interest in criminal defense investigation. Criminal law always sounded like a dark business to be in, and one very far removed from my personal experience . . . until now. I'm standing here just paying the bills until one of my songs hits the big time.

Natman holds a list we read together—addresses we need to visit today—Jamal's mother and a couple of witnesses to the kidnapping at gunpoint. Faintly, coming from behind me, I hear soft, fast-moving tapping sounds. Footsteps . . . someone is running in our direction.

A couple of seconds later, a young black man brushes up

against my right arm and shoulder as he continues quickly past us. I can smell his sweat and his fear. My eyes instantly track his expediently diminishing silhouette moving in a straight line ahead of us, now much further down the sidewalk. The young man is wearing blue jeans, blue T-shirt, and a blue baseball cap . . . black pistol in his right hand waving in the motion of a competitive sprinter.

"Natman, he's got a pistol!" I say, as I look behind me to see who or what he is running from.

"Oh? Does he?" Natman takes a momentary look and then returns his focus to the paper. "This should be her house here on the corner. C'mon. By the way, you need to return that red car and get a neutral color. No blue either. We're in a Crips neighborhood. All blue. Red is the enemy. The Bloods."

What the hell! Why didn't someone bother to tell me this? I'm silent, but as you can imagine, a tidal wave of paranoia surges through my brain. I walk across the street with the attorney, and we knock on the front door and wait for someone to answer.

I'm a blond and blue-eye white person, yet I'm not a complete stranger to this culture. Originally from the New York metro area, having grown up in Long Island and Northern New Jersey, I moved on my own to Brooklyn in my mid-twenties. I worked as a paralegal in an international entertainment company headquartered in Times Square.

Growing up in an angry racial environment during the 1970s, I spent more than one day after middle school running two and a half miles home ahead of the eagerly pursuing black boys and later, as an adult in NYC, honing the trait of minding my own business.

We enter the Shakir residence and talk with mom. Nice, welcoming and grateful lady. She loves her son and appreciates that we are there on his behalf. An hour or so later, we continue with our other interviews for the morning without incident. Joining us for lunch at her beloved M&M's family-style restaurant here in Compton is world-renowned mitigation investigation specialist Scharlette Holdman. M&M's restaurant reminds me of black Harlem in the 1980s.

Scharlette is an older woman currently from San Francisco. Her eyes are warm and welcoming, and her smile is full of life and love. I instantly connect with her.

It has been almost 10 years since I lived in New York City, and I'm out of practice interacting with people of other cultures. Living in Nashville is a far cry from the multi-colored New York metro life. I steady myself; Scharlette is my island of sanctuary in this rough sea of blackness. Since she joined us, there are now three of us white folks in Compton.

"Honey," she engages me, "you need to take that car back right away. You can't be driving a red car in a Crip neighborhood, unless you want to get shot."

"Yes, I will. Thank you. Nice to meet you."

"Okay," she says, "let's eat!"

I have to admit, M&M's is now a favorite food stop of mine. Wow, what amazing cooking. I have the short ribs. We eat with our hands. No one stares at us. Being here really impresses upon me the reality for black people in a "white man's country." I am feeling like the oddball here. This is their world. They deal with this polarity every day in the greater United States. Perspective.

Like one big happy family of 30 or so people, we simply eat our meal. We are too enthralled with the delicious authentic home-style fare to be sidetracked by any racial biases. I'm definitely coming back here on my own.

Jamal Shakir was the defendant in a capital case. A capital case is one where the death penalty is sought due to the heinous nature of the alleged murder or multiplicity of murders. All indigent defendants facing the death penalty in the United States are granted two attorneys.

The term "learned counsel" is used in capital cases to describe the experienced co-counsel who leads the two-attorney defense legal team for a capital defendant. In the Shakir case, Natman Schaye was learned counsel. The associate attorney was a less experienced criminal attorney from the law firm where I worked. If the defendant is indigent (cannot afford to pay for a defense attorney), then taxpayers foot the very large bill.

The average capital process lasts approximately 20 years and costs more than a million dollars. A case I investigated in California not too long ago cost several million to defend. This point alone is food for thought for abolishing the death penalty, not to mention the morality debate over euthanizing physically healthy persons.

There are county, state, and federal public defenders. Either the public defender handles the case in-office or, if they are too busy or the case is a conflict for that office, they hand the case over to private attorneys who are listed on a conflict panel. The conflict panel is a set number of local attorneys who are approved by the court to accept cases that the public defenders cannot handle for whatever reason. The appointed private attorney then enlists the services of their chosen private investigator and motions the court to appoint the investigator on the case.

I am chosen by a private attorney who received a capital case which the public defender could not handle for whatever reason. Then I'm directly appointed by the court to work on the case, and the court authorizes payments to me from federal and/or state funding. Sometimes I receive a payment check from the United States Treasury. My taxes hard at work, paying myself. I like it.

Jamal Shakir was facing 44 counts in his federal indictment, including RICO (Racketeer Influenced and Corrupt Organizations Act), drug trafficking, murder, torture, kidnapping, etc. In this case, "corrupt organizations" mean gangs.

The federal prosecutor tagged Shakir the "kingpin" of the violent Crips gang called "The Rollin' 90s Crips" in Los Angeles and creator of "East Nashville Crips" in Nashville. The case was before the federal court in Nashville because, although he was from Los Angeles, Shakir allegedly used a house in East Nashville as the base of his operations. It was a federal case because allegedly, Shakir's drug ring operated in Los Angeles, Nashville, Memphis, and Oklahoma City with drug runs to Charleston, S.C., and Baton Rouge, LA.

The government accused Shakir of kidnapping, torture, and either carrying them out himself or ordering others to commit many murders. One included the murder of a pregnant mother and her boyfriend in front of their toddler. The toddler, who was also shot in both elbows, survived by drinking toilet water. She was found lying next to her deceased, decaying mother over a week later. These case facts alone were pretty upsetting to me and warranted reconsideration of my involvement in defending Mr. Shakir. However, as a dutiful person, I carried on. Besides, it's only temporary, until I hit the big time in the music business.

Scharlette Holdman was the mitigation investigator for Ted Bundy, Ted Kaczinski (the "Unabomber"), and many other high-profile defendants. Her experience was endless.

Scharlette and I ended up spending considerable time together on my first trip to South Central Los Angeles. She introduced me to two private investigators on her staff who later trained me in gathering court records, and she brought me to the maximum-security state penitentiary to meet Jamal.

She was so motherly to him, and it wasn't fake at all. I just sat back and watched her loving this stranger from a completely different world. She showed incredible compassion for this young man, regardless of what he might have done to others. It was easy to tell he trusted her. Who wouldn't?

The investigators that I worked with on the Shakir case were very experienced and passionate about saving lives. They were good people. They were crusaders against the death penalty. I'm not a crusader by any means. I've never been politically outspoken. I wasn't even against the death penalty back then. One of Scharlette's investigators used to joke that I was probably undercover for the FBI. I wouldn't have minded that back then at all.

Mitigation is a separate area of investigation used to reduce or negate a sentence because of the defendant's special circumstances—mental health or bio-social history, past emotional abuse, brain injury or other variables.

In a capital case, the mitigation goal is to commute the potential death sentence to a life sentence. A mitigation-investigation specialist's primary function and purpose is to prevent persons convicted of crimes from being executed. Holdman is great at her work. I don't believe she considers it a job. She loves her work and loves saving lives.

My involvement on the Shakir case was extremely interesting work. Not only did I fly around the country at my own pace every week, but I learned a great deal about other cultures, the criminal justice system, lawyering and lawyers. I met many fascinating people like Scharlette Holdman along the way. It was a thought-provoking "life university" course on the psychology of people, culture, and perceptions of justice. It also renewed my passion for solving puzzles and exploring concepts.

I've always had an inquisitive mind, much to my mother's dismay. "Because I said so," was often her final answer when I was a young child. She really didn't know the answer to all my questions, and the multitude of them drove her to frustration. I wanted to know how everything worked.

After school, I would disassemble small appliances and put them back together. Sometimes I wondered why so many screws and bolts were needed, so I didn't always put them all back in the unit. I remember having a couple screws left over from reassembling my alarm clock. It still worked fine.

I used to watch *Mission Impossible* on television and pretend I was a secret agent with all the electronic gadgets they used. When no one was home, I would gather pseudo tools (forks, knives, anything metal, whatever) and crawl around behind the sofa running imaginary wires, tapping phones, and planting bugs into live electrical outlets. I learned at a young age about the power of electricity. Ouch.

Though my mother championed the idea of me becoming an attorney, as a child I dreamed of delivering a message of love and light to the world through my songs. If that didn't work out, then life as a carpenter or mechanic would suit me fine. My introduction into actual criminal defense investigation on the Shakir case brought back my youthful inclination for solving problems and fixing things.

I worked on the Shakir case less than a year before leaving the law firm and going out on my own as a criminal defense investigator, so I wasn't involved in the later stages of investigation or the trial. I read online that after an eight-month trial seven years after I worked on the case, Shakir was convicted on 34 counts and ordered to serve 16 life sentences without the opportunity for parole (LWOP).

I don't know what mitigation evidence was presented, but apparently the jury could not unanimously agree on a sentence of death—required to impose the death penalty. That is a big win for the defense team, especially Scharlette. She saved another life.

Working alongside Ms. Holdman and her team, I learned to care for a person that killed, or might have killed, another person—seeing the humanity in them, and affirming that every life matters. This lesson stuck with me and has been an invaluable gift in my work to this day. I also learned that people actually work hard on behalf of homicide defendants to save them from execution. This was really a foreign concept to me.

I never developed a great interest in the mental health aspect of mitigation, which I believe is Scharlette's area of expertise, though I do enjoy investigating a client's personal life history and meeting their family. Investigators like Scharlette and her team are true champions of their cause and their clients. They are top-notch investigators, and I'm very lucky to have begun to learn my new trade from them.

I tell folks I had no formal training before beginning my career as a criminal defense investigator, though I was actually trained on-the-job by three of the very best defense investigators in the country regarding collecting records, basic mitigation, and developing compassion for a death row client. Although having worked on the Shakir case as an investigative paralegal didn't train me for a solo homicide investigation, my experience on this case did train me well to rent only white, silver, or black vehicles whenever I travel to Los Angeles.

MAX ROYBAL: THERE IS NO INSURANCE FOR LIFE

A Kentucky television station received a watermarked jawbone inside a small Tupperware container in the mail. The words, "ONLY FOR ANCHOR CATHERINE DONOVAN," written in large black letters with a magic marker, traversed the bright white mailing label. Was this the remains of missing Fort Campbell, Kentucky's 101 First Airborne Sergeant, Laura Cecere? Indeed it was. This is how the world learned that Laura was dead.

Max Roybal

I identified with Laura because she dove headfirst into a career typically reserved for men. Military aviation was her career choice; private investigation was mine. She was moving up in a man's world. She enjoyed arm wrestling and was strong enough to challenge some of the males. As a competitive armwrestler myself, Laura and I had that in common, too.

Laura was Caucasian, tall, dark, and handsome. She was

married to Max Roybal, a man who had allegedly taken out a $375,000 life insurance policy on her.

Someone murdered Laura and broke her body into pieces. She was fit, popular with the girls, and everyone's all-American. Why would someone kill her? It was all a mystery, and I aimed to solve it. This case haunted me. I tried to summon Laura in my dreams. I wanted her to send me a sign . . . to lead me to her killer and her remains. If I didn't find Laura's skeleton, the world would never know what had happened to her.

Along with the anonymous note to TV Channel 43 were a hand -drawn map and several clues to finding her corpse. Police and many volunteers already had searched for days.

Back in my NYC heyday, there were plenty of serpents around the music industry preying on naive youngsters with big dreams. I moved to Nashville, Tennessee in the mid-1990s to hone my songwriting craft and get a record deal, ignorantly believing that a smaller city would be easier to crack. How wrong I was.

As it turns out, my music had much more traction in NYC. However, there's one reason I'm thankful for the relocation: it led me to one of my soulmates . . . Anne. We were in competition at first sight . . . golf that is. We were both single-digit handicaps, trading wins at our local club. Eventually we became good friends, and later on, committed romantic partners.

Here I am again, naive as ever, standing ankle-deep in riverbed muck searching for a skeleton in this snake-ridden, muddy creek so far out in the countryside on the Tennessee-

Kentucky border that the roads aren't even named. It must be over 100 degrees out here, and the humidity is oppressive. It feels like my skin is melting off my bones and dripping into this skanky creek.

"Eeeeek! Damn!" Another slithery sound crackles through the dry weeds. Instead of the creepy music industry types, these are actual snakes out here in the wild with me! What am I doing, and why didn't I bring a gun?

I don't know why, but for some reason I have always been fearful of backwoods rapists. Right now, I'm hearing the banjo music from *Deliverance* echoing in my head. Must be the heat. My brain is boiling. Many people out here in the boondocks carry guns, and no one would hear me screaming for help.

Anne and I study the hand-drawn map once again. Since law enforcement officers had searched the "exact" location on the map, we decide to hit that same location and then branch off just a bit. Anne and I think we can figure out the subtle clues on the map that police missed.

We walk through the creek where the map indicates Laura Cecere could be found by way of the big blue star on the middle of the torn off paper, but find only chicken wing bones, fish bones, and garbage. I wonder just how intensely police searched. Did they even dig? We brought shovels. Would I even know a small human bone if I found one? Of course, I'm expecting to find her whole skeleton.

No one is around for miles, only the devil and us. Anne is about 25 yards upstream from me. Have I already mentioned that I do not like snakes? Without fail, just when you get comfortable in a sketchy situation something happens to keep you alert. There is a dead silence. I'm relaxed. Then I hear something behind me coming close. Holy crap!!

I'm frozen now, just moving my eyes around 180 degrees and waiting to see the shadow of something in my periphery. Maybe it's merely the breeze blowing garbage my way. My concentration is jarred by a high-pitched scream just up ahead.

"Anne! Are you okay?" I yell out as I revive my legs and run up ahead. I hear nothing. "Anne!" I still get no answer. Running through the dense sand and water, I reach the creek bend and get a glimpse of Anne down in the muck. I guess she tripped or something. "You okay?" I pull her up.

"Yayess, I'm sorry baiby. I keep hearing snakes, and I was fixin' to pick up that bone over there and wasn't watching," she explains in her syrupy southern drawl.

"Yeah, jeez. Let's take a break. It's just another chicken wing."

We sit together at the creek bed, just above the waterline. The banks, sandy and exposed to the weather, are quite high, about five feet up to the grass. It's actually a bit cooler down at this level, sitting with my back against the sandy wall. We take a moment to breathe. Drink some water.

"This is ridiculous. She could be buried anywhere, under the water I'm guessing. We would never notice signs of disturbed earth underneath the water." I go on, "This stupid map could just be a friggin' joke too! I really want to find her. No one deserves to die like she did."

"Yeah, me too," Anne agrees.

A rustling noise draws our attention to the dried brush and twigs a few feet away. "Ahhhh," we both squeak, as I grab her hand. I hate snakes! I do not hate them personally; they can't help looking so poisonous. Those creepy, flickering forked tongues give me the creeps.

This is beginning to remind me of *Ssssss*, a movie I saw when I was 13. A boa constrictor swallowed a man whole, and then a mad scientist turned his niece's boyfriend into a black mamba. It had human eyes and a snake body. Why do I think of such things while I'm out here? Stop. Focus.

"Ugh," I exhale. "Is that one poisonous?" I quizzed Anne.

"I'm not gettin' close enough to answer that," she replies, not attempting to move any closer to investigate.

Of course, now every little sound is going to be a poisonous snake, so I'm making snake noises and having fun with Anne as I wait for an oncoming heat stroke.

"If you're gonna keep doing that shi-at, we're leaving!" Anne scolds me.

"Yeah. Yeah."

"I might shoulda just let you come here on your own!" she says.

"Yes, indeed." I think about it for a second and realize that she's right. "Thanks for coming with me."

For some unknown reason, I take my shovel out and start digging right where I'm standing. As I survey my immediate area, I realize our resting spot is a bit abnormal compared to the other banks. Maybe Laura's giving me a sign. Maybe she made Anne trip and fall right here in this special spot.

A slight rush of adrenaline surges through me. I always feel it in my hands first, like stinging nettles to the back of my wrists. Without saying anything to Anne, I start moving loose rocks and dirt. I think she's napping or meditating anyway. We've been out here a few hours searching in the blazing Tennessee summer sun.

Quietly, I dislodge a good size boulder embedded in the middle of the bank just to my left. This whole area around the boulder seems depressed, as if someone had dug here before and didn't fill it all back in. If bones are here, I do not want to break them with my shovel.

My fingers are getting a little irritated now from scraping away at the rough silt and sand as I excavate manually. I hear some more slithering up above me. I'm going to put away whoever did this to Laura, and to me!

There's nothing. I need to rest a minute. So hot. Dehydrated. Can't breathe. Need water. I lean back against the bank, my eyes surveying the situation in front of me. Anne's eyes are closed, a water bottle balanced in her hand.

Still trying to interpret the map, racking my brain for some answers, scenarios, and clues to pop off the paper. I try to summon Laura inside my head.

"Laura, tell me where you are!" I demand. I close my eyes and practice my spiritual energy work. Moving myself into her energy to know what she knows. I relate to Laura. We might have been friends. I sit back again and moan in frustration, and I keep trying with my mind to solve this homicide.

To my left, where I have been digging and moving the surface of the creek bank, a trickle of sand falls. To be expected. I've disturbed it. I don't even turn to look. I'm tired. I'm still deep in concentration trying to summon Laura. More sand spills down next to me. Whatever. I turn slightly to look at Anne on the other side of me, thinking we should get out of here. The sun is going down. More sand moves.

"Aaahhh!" I scream inside my head. Something is touching my shoulder! Now it is touching my neck! Is it a snake? Frozen, I move my eyes to the left.

Phew, no. Breathe. It is just a stick or something touching me that must have come down in the sand. All of a sudden, a lot of sand starts moving as if the whole bank is falling down into the creek. I can feel my eyebrows come together into a scowl and my eyes intensely focusing as I turn my chin to look over my left shoulder.

I exclaim, "Skull! Eyes! It is moving. Laura?"

Startled, Anne jumps up. It's not a stick; it's a skeleton bone on my shoulder. Frantic and disheveled, I bounce up from the sand. "Aaaahhh," I yell, unable to control my inner child who's still afraid of the dark.

Anne wakes me from my frightening lucid dream. While we had, in fact, spent the day trenching through snake-ridden muck searching for Laura's remains, I did not find her skeleton. That part happened only in my dream. I had fallen asleep, exhausted, after returning home from our search.

Welcome to the nightmare of homicide investigation. I call it a nightmare, but that's only true for those of us who actually care about our cases.

When I'm involved on a case, working it, I live and breathe it.

Max Roybal: Writing on the Wall

After deciding to leave my paralegal position at the law firm and becoming an independent criminal defense investigator, my first solo homicide case investigation happened right off the bat. Practically the moment I gained my Tennessee private investigator license, an investigator working with the federal defender's office recommended me to Nashville attorney Michael Terry, of the legal firm Terry & Gore.

This investigator didn't know me, but he somehow heard I was now licensed and phoned me. I don't remember how he acquired my name and number. I joined him at Brown's Diner, his favorite hamburger joint. He wanted to meet me and get a feel for what I was all about personally.

Within a couple of days attorney Michael Terry called, saying he needed an investigator on a homicide case and I came recommended. Terry interviewed me and hired me on the spot.

Again, I'm not sure why. I had no experience investigating murder, though I already had a couple of sexual assault witness interviews under my belt with good results. I was nervous meeting Mr. Terry because I was so green in my professional experience. Of course, I wanted the case, and apparently I interviewed well enough.

The defendant, Max Roybal, was charged with two murders: Max's former girlfriend, Karen Anderson, and his current wife, Laura Cecere, who died several years apart. I started out investigating Roybal's two homicide cases using my familiar methods—reviewing and organizing the file. Mr. Terry invited me to work out of his office and pointed me to a large box of case documents.

Later that week, I started by organizing and understanding the file. This entailed reading every piece of paper multiple times, digesting the information, and creating notes. I wrote out my theories, questions, people I wanted to look into, research I wanted to do about events or issues, and a "to do" list. In addition, I created a timeline of case-related events.

My files contained information on the background and family lives of the main players in the case: Max, Laura, and Karen. I created a witness list that included information on each witness's relevance and connection with the victims or Max, inconsistencies of witness statements, perceived untruths, or mistaken comments by witnesses. I cross-referenced every page of discovery on both alleged homicides.

In the beginning of a criminal case, the defense attorney receives "discovery" from the prosecution. It includes all elements of the police investigation that led to the arrest of the defendant. Discovery should include police incident and supplemental reports (including photographs and audiovisual recordings), death certificate, witness statements, forensic reports and photographs (including autopsy), and the criminal history of the defendant and possibly alleged victim(s).

Discovery must also include any and all information police uncovered that points to the defendant's innocence. Unfortunately, they forget to give us these documents sometimes.

I believe the discovery on these cases filled a banker's box, which is perhaps 15 inches of papers if piled vertically.

Some of the witnesses the State of Tennessee questioned were relevant to both cases, while others were not. I'm extremely thorough. I copy every page that mentions a name and place it into a folder with that name on it, and place a copy in a folder with that date on it. I also place a copy in a folder with the topic or event on it.

This method ensures that a copy of any document relating to a person or event can easily be found together with other relevant documents. For me, this is the most effective way to organize a criminal file for defense team members. They can peruse the files and never get lost or miss a connection between people or events in the discovery.

This activity took about 25 hours and generated an additional banker's box of organized copies, plus myriad summaries and notes. All of the original discovery documents are kept in their original place, as if undisturbed, in the original file box labeled "discovery."

I follow this process on every case, large or small. Strangely enough, I love this aspect of my work. I love the paperwork. I love finding the clues in the documents, the incongruities. I love finding the loopholes in prosecution theories, the missing pieces of the paper puzzle. I do not consider it boring at all.

I love words: how they're used, what they mean in the

context of a document or conversation, and how certain people convey their ideas. I enjoy things stated clearly. Unraveling the convoluted styles of people's talk is a puzzle-solving skill and a task I enjoy.

Police investigation documents can reveal errors of logic and bias. In addition, these documents can reveal where detectives lead a witness. These documents show what police did . . . and what they failed to do. It's true that the devil is always in the details.

Unfortunately, sometimes the defense must fight to obtain the discovery. This might come as a surprise, but prosecutors don't always play fair. In addition, the criminal justice system in the United States is set up to favor the prosecution with regard to investigative resources. Prosecutors have the benefit of the entire police force and district attorney office investigators. They also have access to government documents that the defense is not entitled to, unless they are turned over to the defense by the district attorney or attorney general.

While it is said that the justice system favors the defendant by placing the burden of proof on the prosecution, that's only a question before the jury at the end of trial. The entire defense investigation is hampered by limited access to important information that only the prosecution is allowed to obtain.

For example, I cannot access some DMV records, bank records, police records relating to other parties, medical records, psychological records, social services records, etc. For the most part, any document created by the government is not accessible to the defense unless the prosecutor hands it over, or the court issues a subpoena.

There is a drawback to seeking a subpoena: the defense is showing its hand to the prosecution prior to trial, thereby allowing the prosecution to learn about their defense strategy. The prosecution then has the added benefit of knowing which documents have been sought by defense, which might not already be in the prosecution's possession, as the prosecutor might not have thought to ask for them.

Also, because of legislated confidential items falling under HIPAA (Health Insurance Portability and Accountability Act, 1996), unless the source turns documents over voluntarily, the defense team can only ask the court to allow access to this personal and private information. The court will then obtain the records "in camera," meaning the courts reviews the documents first and determines whether or not the documents are relevant to the case. If they are relevant, then the court will provide the documents to the defense team and prosecution.

The defense is restricted as to what evidence can be presented to jurors in as far as it relates to prior crimes, associations, and habits of the victim. Thus, before juries decide the question of guilt or innocence, they don't always have the luxury of hearing all the available evidence. This aspect of the system is set up to protect the alleged victim from prejudice.

My concern is that the government (the prosecutor) has access to more information than does the defense. Prosecution also has access to numerous investigative personnel, while defense is typically granted one investigator (unless it's a capital case) and a very limited budget on indigent cases.

Returning to the case at hand . . . as it turned out, Max

Roybal was only a partial beneficiary of the life insurance policy on Laura Cecere. Laura's family members were also beneficiaries, and the proceeds would be split among them and Max.

The attorneys and I met often and talked about the case in their office, over team lunches and social gatherings. Mr. Terry and his legal partner Ms. Gore are wonderful, intelligent people that I enjoy knowing on a personal basis.

Being able to speak with a case attorney candidly and frequently is a major contributing factor to working effectively and comprehensively on any case. This was a great experience for my first whole-case endeavor.

I lived and dreamed about the Roybal cases for many months. Those who believed in Max's innocence seemed to be in the minority. The deaths of Anderson and Cecere happened in a rural county north of Nashville. Max wasn't native to the area, but was an outsider from the Southwest United States. He was quiet and unassuming while Laura was popular and in a high-profile military position as a female Sergeant in the 101st Airborne Division.

Laura's disappearance and later assumed death was big news for a small town, and the media actively reported information about Max's charges in both the Anderson and Cecere homicides.

I met Max in his cell at Montgomery County Jail. He told me he couldn't afford to pay bail, and that he was anxious for trial so he could be released. He professed his innocence all along, and his daughter supported him whole-heartedly. He came across to me as overconfident and perhaps manipulative.

Defendants whom I judge as guilty often cause me to feel as if they think they are fooling me. They believe I can't see through them. They believe they're smarter than I am. I'm just a dumb blonde to them, I suppose. Max didn't treat me that way. He was respectful and appreciative, but still I had an uneasy feeling about him.

He was an odd sort of person, and often that quality can land folks in jail. If someone was quiet, like Max, and not from the area, and therefore spoke or thought differently, local folks were more likely to be suspicious. Max was very businesslike and was focused on getting things done, and yet he was reserved at the same time. He didn't like talking about other people

He really didn't even want to talk about Laura, and I could tell he somehow wanted this ordeal to be over without bothering or involving anyone else.

How was I supposed to investigate this case? Did Max have an alibi? Did others have motive and opportunity? Why did someone mail the jawbone to the television station? Several thoughts crossed my mind; either someone was messing with us, or felt guilty, or needed Laura's body to be found for whatever reason. Maybe someone needed to prove she was dead. Perhaps just a piece of Laura's body was enough to fulfill their intention.

With regard to collecting life insurance, there is a waiting period before benefits are dispersed in cases of a missing person. In case of actual death, financial benefit comes quickly.

In this case, why tell us where the rest of the body was if only for life insurance? Not necessary, because the jawbone was proof of death. So why were the map and the letters with clues toward finding Laura's remains sent? Since Max was a local stranger, in a marriage of convenience with Laura, and a beneficiary of her life insurance, her jawbone showing up clearly shed a lot of suspicion upon him.

I began my fieldwork investigation by visiting the Air Assault School in Fort Campbell, Kentucky. Laura was an instructor there. I drove from Fort Campbell to Laura's residence. The distance was approximately eight miles. Someone had found Laura's dogs inside her home on Saturday morning—the day after her disappearance—which meant she came home after work and let them in.

I talked to neighbors, roommates, and girlfriends past and present. She had gone out to the local girls' bar Friday night, after which she was never seen again. The last concrete evidence of her whereabouts was on a Wal-Mart ATM video about 7:30 p.m. that Friday evening.

Laura's best friend Gayle told me that Laura was raped on the base in Saudi Arabia, perhaps by her supervisor, a non-commissioned Officer (NCO). I heard the same thing from her other friends. Actually, I was told she might have been raped twice. I've read that rape of U.S. military women overseas by our own service members is disgustingly common.

It was clear that men wanted Laura. They didn't know she was gay. If they did, they probably would have wanted her even more.

Gayle helped Laura come up with a story about being married to a man in another state so that men would leave her alone. Some people suggested Max Roybal might have wanted Laura, too. Everyone agreed she and Max were good friends. They married for mutual benefit—a marriage of convenience.

This helped Laura fend off men on the base, and she could live off-base herself. Max received military benefits from the marriage.

Gayle told me that Laura spent time with Max when she was depressed. When Laura was found to be missing, Gayle and Max searched for her together. Gayle also confided to me that military investigations personnel questioned her thoroughly and tried to sway her into believing Max was guilty early on. Though they didn't let go of their witch-hunt, she never bought into it. Thus, Laura's best friend believed that Max was innocent.

Gayle welcomed my interviews, which also told me that she trusted Max. She told me that Laura liked Max and that they got along famously. After all, no woman would marry just any man and trust him with her personal life. I quoted Laura's closest friend in my notes: "I wasn't there, so I don't know, but in my heart, Max would not do this to Laura."

I then spoke to friends of Max who said they were at Max's house on the night Laura disappeared, watching a boxing match on TV—or was it the night before? That was one of the problems with interviewing people four years after the fact.

Max's friends confirmed that he was friends with Laura, and they swore up and down he would never do something so evil. There were simply no ill feelings between Max and Laura to be found. Also, Max had a good job and wasn't hurting for money. Laura's family, on the other hand, was experiencing financial challenges.

There was a daunting cloud hanging over Laura named Patrick, her father. Apparently, he was somewhat aggressive with her mother, and Laura had a dangerous habit of stepping in between them. Patrick did not like the fact that Laura was gay. There was also rumor that he was attracted to Laura.

Laura wanted her mother to leave Patrick for some time. She was disgusted with him. Eventually Laura's mother did leave Patrick, and the Ceceres' divorce and fights over money were stressful for both Laura and her mother. All of these things were going on when Laura disappeared, and Laura had named her mother, father, and Max as beneficiaries of her $375,000 life insurance policy. She left enough for all of them.

Max told me that Patrick showed up at Max's house the week before the television station received Laura's jawbone. Patrick left a sticky note on Max's door saying that he wanted Laura's four-wheeler. Laura was missing at the time, but no one knew she was dead.

Laura's best friend also told me that it was 100 percent Laura's idea to include Max on her life insurance. She was in the military. She was married to Max, albeit in a marriage of convenience. If something happened to her, Max would not lose his house. In this way, Laura was taking care of Max of her own accord. No one ever told me that Max asked for the life insurance.

Laura was in a relationship with a woman named Conner at the time of her disappearance. This fact was supported by Conner and others. Conner could not reach Laura by phone that entire weekend. She drove by Laura's house looking for her, but Laura wasn't there. Laura's dogs were inside the house.

I also talked to Laura's ex-girlfriends, and there were several. Back in the mid-1990s, "Don't Ask, Don't Tell" was the motto of the military. Being gay was not okay. It had to be hidden.

Max's daughter confided to me that Max was very protective of Laura's personal life. He didn't divulge to others that she was gay, even though Laura was popular with the women on base. They loved Laura. Perhaps some of them loved her a little too much.

Laura's known ex-girlfriends told me about a stalker chick who fantasized about being in a relationship with Laura but never was. It seemed unlikely that Laura would have been in a relationship with this woman. Laura was tall, strong, pretty, and popular, as were all of her known girlfriends. This stalker—I'll call her Devilia for the sake of preserving her identity and possible innocence—was a "clinger-on" type. She probably had some mental health issues. Several women described her as being very strange, hopelessly in love with Laura, and obsessive.

Investigating Devilia as an "alternate suspect" (a person capable of perpetrating the crime) became a priority for me. Whenever I come across a person that has motive and opportunity to commit the crime charged to my guy, of course I investigate that person fully. I pull court records to learn about the person's civil and criminal histories. I ask questions about them, and if possible, interview them directly.

Needless to say I had to find out more about Devilia. So after speaking with Laura's friends, I spoke with Devilia's ex-girlfriend Stacey. Exes are typically a very rich source of information, and often are willing to talk. It turned out that Devilia's ex-girlfriend was more than willing to talk to me. Stacey described Laura as outgoing and fun to be around. She remembered seeing Max at Laura's memorial with a woman believed to be Laura's mother. Her experiences with Devilia were very interesting, to say the least.

Stacey met Devilia at the girls' bar—the same bar where Laura was last seen. They dated for about a year and a half, during which time they lived together. Stacey described Devilia as jealous, possessive, suicidal, and homicidal. She said Devilia experienced dramatic mood swings, and had a "special place," a secret place, where she went to gather her thoughts.

After learning from friends that Devilia cheated on her, Stacey kicked her out. Devilia was not at all happy about it. She stalked Stacey, and Stacey considered filing a restraining order against her, but never did.

Devilia's family history was dark and depressive. She was taking anti-depressants, steroids, and painkillers. Stacey told me that Devilia attempted suicide around the time Laura disappeared. Also, Devilia often went away for up to a month at a time, and was "missing in action" during the time someone sent Laura's jawbone to the TV station.

The night Laura disappeared, Stacey went to the girls' bar and recalled seeing Devilia talking to Laura at the bar. Afterward Devilia showed no emotion about Laura's disappearance. Stacey told me that it was completely possible that Devilia killed Laura. She said she wouldn't be surprised at anything.

I called Devilia and invited her to lunch.

I sit at a front table at a local pub in Devilia's town at around noon on a Tuesday, mentally preparing myself as I wait for her to arrive. She knows to search the room for a tall, thin, blonde woman sitting alone. My table allows me to see everyone who walks into the restaurant.

This short, out of shape, overconfident woman stands in the doorway. Her eyes land on me. I smile and wave her over to the table. I act very happy to meet her and turn on the charm from the first moment, flirting with her. She loves it.

I order my favorite modified grilled Ruben—nothing but meat and extra cheese—and a beer, as well as a cheeseburger and beer for her. She tells me stories of her three-year monogamous, romantic relationship with Laura. This is an obvious lie, since I've already learned from others and Devilia's ex-girlfriend that she lived with Stacey.

I sit there nodding and chomping on my Ruben, interjecting useless questions and empty compliments in order to keep her talking. She talks about Laura wanting to kill herself so that her family could get the insurance money. Devilia also tells me that she and Laura had a suicide pact, but Laura must have gone through with it without her. She talks about a "secret place" she and Laura would go four-wheeling and camping out on someone's vast acreage just over the Kentucky border. She says she didn't attend Laura's funeral because it would've been too hard on her.

Devilia expresses tremendous love for Laura. Why didn't she keep her promise to commit suicide with her beloved Laura? Why leave Laura alone in that? She answers my questions, saying she's not that kind of person. I think to myself, didn't you just tell me you had an agreement with Laura to do so? Okay, big inconsistency here.

She goes on to tell me that Max was in love with Laura but wasn't supposed to be. I ask her if Max loved Laura more than her, and she gives me a very emphatic, "NO!" She tells me that Laura's father, Patrick, hit Laura during an argument he was having with her mother, and that he would be a person of interest to me.

I ask her to take me to Laura's and her secret place.

"Nah, can't do that," she answers.

"No? Too special, I guess, huh?"

"Oh, yeah, definitely. It's just up over the border north of Fort Campbell about an hour and a half drive from here," she says vaguely. "A friend has a lot of land up there."

I suddenly have a feeling that we might find Laura's body in that "secret place."

She goes on. "Laura didn't like sharing me with anyone. I don't think she'd like me showing anyone our special place."

"Right. I understand." I keep working on her, but she won't give it up. She's demented.

Considering what other people have already told me about Devilia, I can see they were right on. She's an obsessive, delusional, stalker. She has some mental health issues, for certain.

"Hey," I say, "Thanks for meeting with me." I give her a hug. "I know this was really hard on you. I have your number. Is it okay if I call you if I have any questions I forgot to ask?"

"Yeah, sure!" She smiles devilishly. "Glad I could help. Nice meeting you too. You should look into Patrick and Max," she adds matter-of-factly, trying to move my focus away from her.

"Right on. Thank you!" I say. I think to myself, you just said Laura committed suicide, so why should I look at anyone else? So maybe Laura bought a lot of life insurance so that she could take care of Max and her family, and then killed herself.

Before her death Laura had been reassigned to a station in Korea. No one believed she was unhappy or upset about going overseas. Devilia even told me that Laura was fine with heading off to Korea. Other friends told me Laura accepted the post and was resigned to her duty overseas.

I could not help but feel during our long conversation that Devilia could be Laura's killer. Creepy shit. Snake! Of course, she might just be lonely and disturbed — not a killer.

I was also thinking, however, that Laura could take Devilia down in an instant, so she must have hit Laura in the head or something. Maybe she shot her. Perhaps Laura's body was broken in pieces, cut up, and only the jawbone was mailed. Can a person live without their lower jaw? A prosecution expert said no. I told the defense attorneys that I thought I knew who killed Laura, but then again, there were other alternate suspects as well.

One witness failed the polygraph when police officers asked if he knew where they could find Laura's body. The police told him they were not interested in him; they just wanted Max. This witness was a friend of Max's.

I talked with this man one day about his police interrogation. He led me down into his basement apartment underneath a store just a few blocks from the jail and the justice building where Max awaited his day in court. He was scared to talk with me, and I was scared to be in that dark basement alone with him. He and his wife ran a business together, and they lived with their two children in this small, squat underground apartment. Police learned that Max had loaned him money in the past.

It turned out that he had nothing to offer on the case, but police hounded him anyway and kept trying to get him to point the finger at Max. He told me that during their search of his apartment, the Tennessee Bureau of Investigations (local FBI) took his passport without telling him and told him not to leave town.

My notes quoted him as saying, "The police can do whatever they want. I'd rather take my chances with the terrorists."

Keep two things in mind: honest people fail polygraphs every day just because they're nervous, and some police know how to scare the hell out of innocent folks.

Still more suspects surfaced during my investigation. There was a rumor that Laura might have attended a party at a nearby apartment complex that Friday night. Her truck was found on that street. A man who trained female runners at Fort Campbell hosted the party. Maybe it was a surprise party for two! My research indicated that he had served time as a sex offender. What? I could find no solid ties between Laura and this man, so this was a dead end. Who knows who was with Laura in her last hours?

It could have been some other guy. She had been assaulted before by male colleagues. Laura had an affair with the wife of a military sergeant. The sergeant got into a public fistfight with one of Laura's girlfriends at some point before his wife began sending Laura steamy letters. Did he find out?

Last, but not least, I inquired about Susan Spitman. She was a police detective investigating Laura's disappearance and later homicide. Spitman was rumored to have socialized with Laura in the past. She took Laura's truck into evidence and later drove the truck to Laura's funeral, ostensibly to give to Laura's mother.

She made many interesting comments of a more personal nature to Laura's friends when interviewing them. She "admired" Laura. Max told me that Spitman sat next to Laura's mother at the funeral and when the rest of Laura's family arrived, Spitman did not relinquish her seat to them. He also overheard Spitman call Laura's mother, "mom."

I called Spitman's home to set up an interview and a woman answered saying she wasn't home. I was able somehow to get someone at the police station from which she had now retired to tell me she left due to issues surrounding emotional instability. I never interviewed her, but I didn't need to at this point. Our defense team could surmise whatever we wanted, and present our version to the jury.

After approximately eight months of investigation, I had probably talked to more than 30 people. I had looked into the backgrounds of multiple alternate suspects and developed theories about how any one of them could have killed Laura.

Attorneys Terry & Gore were ready for court, but they were still concerned about one prosecution witness in particular who had stated that Max asked her about autopsies and collecting life insurance prior to Laura's jawbone making the news.

Allegedly, Max asked interesting questions regarding how long one had to wait to file an insurance claim, and whether proof of death must be shown if someone was missing. The prosecution's theory would be that Max took out life insurance policies on people who subsequently ended up dead.

In addition, the Tupperware in which the jawbone had been packaged matched the Tupperware in Max's house. Moreover, the prosecution would focus on the statement by the woman who said Max asked her about autopsies and collecting life insurance.

I interviewed this woman; let's call her Susan Craft. She and Max used to be work friends. When Ms. Craft was initially questioned by police, she didn't mention these most interesting alleged facts: that Max had asked her about autopsies and life insurance. She only mentioned them many months later during a follow-up interview by military investigators. Still, it was pretty damaging stuff . . . if true. None of us were certain how to impeach her or what angle to take if she testified at trial.

Max Roybal: Digging Up Bodies

After Laura's jawbone was mailed to the TV station, law enforcement discovered that Max's former girlfriend Karen, who was only in her 30s, was also deceased. They exhumed Karen's body and examined for manner of death a second time.

Karen Anderson was a mentally challenged person on whom Max took out life insurance. There was no smoking gun; no Tupperware, no jawbone, and no clues or maps mailed to local TV personalities. There were also no emotionally unfit lead detectives, angry and jealous fathers, sexual assaults by colleagues, stalking, or outgoing lifestyles.

While the Laura Cecere case was sensationalized in the media, the Karen Anderson case received much less press. Karen lived at home, by herself, and Max took care of her.

Apparently, when Max wasn't around, Karen's uncle also "took care" of her sexually. She died in 1994 of "natural causes" according to the police incident report. I believe what the officer meant to say was that her death was not suspicious and that she appeared to have died in a natural manner. The medical examiner found blunt force trauma to be the cause of death, theorizing she fell and hit her head. After Laura Cecere was murdered in 1997, the State of Tennessee dug up Karen's body and now concluded she was also murdered—by Max.

Cause of death and manner of death can be confusing. "Cause of death" is the injury that caused a person to die, i.e., blunt force trauma to the head. "Manner of death" is how the cause of death was incurred, i.e., homicide.

The prosecution's medical examiner was going to testify that Karen had blunt force trauma injury to the brain and had been murdered. The defense needed a medical examiner expert to testify that Karen's manner of death was natural, and that although she had a head injury, there was no evidence as to an unnatural cause of the injury. She had fallen and hit her head. You could say that the manner of death was in question, since head trauma is often not the result of homicide but of an accident or fall.

The rookie police officer first on the scene of Karen's death wrote the following in his incident report: "It appears the subject died of natural causes."

How would he know that? She was dead on the floor and there was nothing seemingly out of place. That was all he could have possibly observed. There were no witnesses at the scene. His report was good for the defense. An official person, a trained police officer, said it wasn't a homicide. Likewise, the original medical examiner reported he saw nothing suspicious and no reason to believe another person caused Karen's death. Did he read the police report before reaching his conclusions? Certainly he did. It is very typical for a medical examiner to consult the police reports for evidence which will help determine the manner of death.

I really didn't do much investigation in this case except to interview two witnesses and bring them to trial: our medical examiner expert and the scene cop. I called the State's (prosecution's) medical examiner to ask about Karen's autopsy and whether there was anything unusual in his findings.

I cannot remember the specific questions I asked him, but I remember his replies: "I work on dead people! That's what I do! What do you want to know?" He answered every question in an angry manner. This case was tried on plausible theories of forensics and the testimony of four witnesses. Max would not be taking the stand in his own defense.

I knew I had to get the cop to testify in court. This was my first homicide case, so I didn't really know how all this stuff was supposed to play out, but I didn't think the guy was going to talk to me. I was working for the other side . . . the "dark" side. In the minds of the police, I help set criminals free. I undo all the work they did. Okay, how was I going to do this?

I knock on the front door of his residence. No answer. It's about three in the afternoon.

At 4:00 p.m. I try again. Still there's no answer at the officer's house. I grab a bite to eat. At six o'clock in the evening, there's still no answer at the officer's house. It's getting dark outside and I don't want to bother a witness at night. It scares them. It scares me too.

I wait in the black and gold special edition 280-Z sports car that my father won in a golf tournament. He had given it to me after he moved on from driving it. My father had the good fortune of living out his childhood dream as a professional golfer. Actually, he earned that good fortune through hard work and determination—with the support of a great woman by his side. My Mom often worked two jobs and took care of the kids while he was off touring.

My father was a club pro who played in many tournaments . . . and seemed to win a lot. He would periodically bring a new car home throughout my high school years—a couple of which I crashed while falling asleep at the wheel. But lo and behold, another first place automobile would appear. I love driving fast, so his gift of the 280-Z was lovely. After that one died of old age, my mother gave me her matching red one. Smile.

Still parked across the street from the officer's house, I wait some more. It's really dark at 9:05 p.m. A small dark SUV finally pulls into his driveway and goes around to the back of his house.

I give him a few minutes to get into the house and turn the lights on. No lights come on. I walk up onto the dark front porch and knock on the door. No one answers. Still no lights on in the house. I knock again. Nothing.

I walk around to the back of the house where I can see him and a woman inside the garage unloading groceries from the car. I step lightly down the long driveway and ease into his garage.

"Excuse me, sir?"

"Yeah?" he says, startled.

"I'm sorry to bother you at this hour, but I really need to talk with you for just a few minutes. I'm a private investigator." I show him my state issued wallet-size investigation license.

"Go to the front door. I'll be there in a few minutes," he

says.

Is he blowing me off? Is he going to lock up the garage and leave me standing out there?

The front door opens. All the lights in the house are still off except for a room in the back. It must be the light from the kitchen because I can hear someone putting away groceries. He invites me inside and offers me a seat in the dark living room. Without ever turning on a light, he instructs me to speak quietly. I don't think he wants anyone to see me in his house.

"What do you need to talk with me about?" he inquires.

I explain who I am and why I'm there. I want to know why he wrote that Karen Anderson died of natural causes, so I give him a copy of his police report. He reads it.

"Yeah, I didn't think anything suspicious happened," he responds.

I ask him some questions about how Karen was found and about the state of her home.

After spending a few minutes describing the scene, he confides, "Can we speak off the record?"

Before I can answer, he goes on to tell me . . .

"If anyone killed her, it was her uncle. I know the family, and I've always thought the uncle was very strange and was controlling over her."

Oh, wow. The deeper you dig, the more gold you are apt to mine. I'm glad I sat in my car for six hours!

"Oh, really?" I urge him on.

"Yeah, rumor has it her uncle was having sex with her. I don't think Mr. Roybal is guilty," he concluded.

Pay dirt! "Ahh, yes, I've heard that rumor."

"Yeah, I don't want to be involved in this. You have my report. I don't know if she died of natural causes or if the uncle did it."

"So why, again, did you write that statement?" I quiz him.

"It was my first death incident. I just started as a police officer. I should have written it differently," he admits.

"Right. Well, that's understandable. You wrote what you saw and what you believed at the time. It's all good. You're not in trouble for anything. No one is scrutinizing you. The medical examiner agreed with you, and they buried her. I'm only here to understand the situation."

I want him to relax, all the while knowing we are now going to subpoena him to testify in court.

Thankfully, while he was on the stand at trial this police officer didn't hold back and told the jury everything he told me. He was a good man. He was honest in the face of professional criticism. He testified in support of Max. The jury believed him because it was clear he was humble and forthcoming. He even said he thought Karen's uncle killed her! He described the uncle as an alcoholic pervert and said everyone knew it.

It is typically a great day at trial whenever law enforcement testifies on behalf of the defendant. The jury loved him.

We put the uncle on the stand too. The jury hated him. We won. The jury acquitted Roybal of all charges related to Karen's death.

CASES IN THE NEWS
Adrian Thomas

Four-month-old Matthew Thomas was rushed to the hospital by his father Adrian Thomas after finding him unresponsive. During the interrogation, investigators told Adrian that it had been proven the child died from blunt force trauma and that they knew someone in the household had done it. They threatened to arrest his wife if he did not confess. He was convicted of second degree murder on the basis of his confession.

It was later determined that the cause of death was sepsis (a life-threatening bacterial infection) and the child's death was not a homicide.[5]

Thomas' conviction was unanimously overturned by a court of appeals six years later. "The justices, in a 7-0 decision... cited heavy-handed tactics used by Troy [N.Y.] investigators, who interrogated Thomas for almost nine hours before he demonstrated how he threw the child."[6]

Max Roybal: Rose-Colored Tupperware

We went to separate trials on Max Roybal's homicide charges. Somehow, defense attorney Terry convinced the judge to separate the charges so that Max could get two fair trials, without the prejudice of two murder charges before the jury. The judge even agreed to bring in a jury from outside the county for the second of the two trials.

The jury acquitted Max on the Karen Anderson murder charge. Next, we faced the second jury on the murder of Laura Cecere. Admittedly, this case was much more convoluted and complex, given the large number of witnesses and the four-year span of law enforcement investigation.

As I drove to court for the first day of Max's second murder trial, it dawned on me that months ago while at the military base looking through the military investigation file, I had noticed a placard on an office door in the investigation unit as I walked the hall. The last name on the placard was Craft. This just popped into my head on the way to court. Then I remembered my interview with Ms. Craft at her home. Her husband came into the room, looked me over, and left. He was definitely military.

I phoned ahead to defense attorney Terry on his cell. He

was in the courtroom setting up his files and gearing himself up for court. I told him I had a hunch that this woman might be married to one of the military investigators at Ft. Campbell. Those people apparently wanted really badly to pin Laura's death on Max.

This was the only witness that Max's defense attorneys dreaded because we had no dirt on her. This is the witness who says Max asked her about collecting life insurance and proof of death. She was definitely bad news for Max. The defense strategy was not to cross-examine her at all; instead, the defense attorneys wanted to get her off the stand as quickly as possible. Terry thanked me for calling, but still wasn't sure he wanted to poke around anywhere with her unless we were certain.

Before entering the courtroom, I ran into Laura's mother in the women's restroom. I just knew it was her mother. Who else could it be? Pain and sadness covered this woman's face.

As I washed my hands, my eyes teared up just a bit and I told her I was so sorry for her loss. I looked at her when I spoke, but then looked down, ready to leave the room quickly. She knew I meant it and thanked me, not knowing who I was. She had no idea that I was helping defend the man she believed to have mutilated her daughter. I really wanted to hug her, but all I could do was hurt her even deeper in the hours to come. I gave a sincere smile of condolence and left the restroom.

I sat down at defense counsel table in the courtroom, which is typically reserved exclusively for lawyers. Now Ms. Cecere knew who I was. She probably thought I was a defense attorney.

Michael Terry wanted me by his side at the counsel table because I knew every aspect of the case. His legal partner Ms.

Gore sat in the first row of the audience behind Max and me. I could help with questions for the cross-examination of prosecution witnesses. I had interviewed them. I could help with defense theory and focus. I knew the case inside and out. Gore handed me notes periodically as well.

In the midst of an intense, high-profile homicide trial, I found myself often chuckling inside my head at my new friend Michael Terry. When not looking through them, Terry placed his reading glasses not on his head but up on his forehead just above his eyebrows. He would move them down over his eyes to look at his notes, and then raise them just above his big brown English eyebrows again when he asked a question of a witness. This went on for hours as he worked the courtroom.

This would be a huge "tell" if he were a poker player. He would walk over to the jury box while asking a question, secure his glasses magically to his forehead, and gesture to the jury with a raised eyebrow anticipating the answer, then walk away moving the glasses over his eyeballs to review the next question. Terry's eyebrows said it all; they were his most expressive facial gesture. The rest of his face was deadpan.

I wondered how the glasses stayed in place without resting on his nose, just sort of floating over his eyebrows. He is obviously a magician.

Terry used the impeachment evidence I had given him and tore through each of the state's witnesses. A magician he was. He made all the prosecution witnesses vanish.

During his cross-examination of Laura's father Patrick, Terry implicated him as an alternate suspect for the reasons I stated earlier in addition to his collapsing financial situation and divorce. This tactic outraged the family.

We alleged, by carefully cross-examining prosecution witnesses, that there were multiple other suspicious persons with motive and opportunity to kill Laura. The prosecution put on witness after witness that Terry tore apart with the impeachment evidence, one by one. Impeachment evidence, by the way, is evidence which intimates or clearly proves that a witness is biased, mistaken, lying, or lacks knowledge.

This was a case based entirely on circumstantial evidence. Mere inference. There was no physical evidence tying Max Roybal to the crime, no fingerprints, no hairs, no fibers, no DNA, no smoking guns . . . nothing but conjecture.

The prosecution's theory focused on Max's supposed motive and opportunity, the insurance money, and the inappropriate questions about autopsies and collecting on the insurance that he had allegedly asked. Because a jury acquitted Max of Karen's death, the prosecution was not allowed to mention that case. At this point in the trial, they had nothing because we had blown their witnesses all to pieces. The only witness left was Ms. Craft.

Defense attorney Terry took a chance after my earlier inference and cross-examined her. "Are you married to military investigator Craft?" He asked.

We all held our breath.

Before district attorney Bieber could object, we heard a quick, "Yes, I am," from the witness.

'Yeah baby', I screamed in my mind. I seriously thought I could hear Terry's brain, Gore's brain, and Anne's brain all screaming the same triumphant words. This was the final witness we needed to impeach.

"How long have you been married to Mr. Craft?" he followed up.

"Four months."

"So when you first gave a statement to police you didn't mention that Max was asking about autopsies and insurance, but now since you've been married to a CID (military criminal investigations division) investigator you added those tidbits to enhance your prior statement, correct?"

"Yes, I didn't remember until later."

"No further questions of this witness," Terry gloated, poised his glasses over his happy eyebrows, and nodded at me for a job well done.

The judge excused the witness and the prosecution rested its case. The judge ordered a short recess before the defense was to begin presenting its rebuttal case (put on defense witnesses).

Upon the judge's return to the bench, he began a brief soliloquy on the definition of reliable evidence. I wasn't sure where he was going with this speech. This was my first time in a criminal courtroom.

Max sat front and center between Mr. Terry and me at the attorney table. The district attorney sat at the table to our right. Laura's mother and her ex-girlfriends who had testified sat behind him, along with other friends. Max's daughter, attorney Gore, and my partner Anne sat behind us. There were also some media persons in the back of the room.

The judge continued narrowing down his short lecture about lack of evidence and the prosecution's duty to bring a real case to court. Now my ears perked up. Terry's glasses came off completely and could be heard across the quiet room crashing onto the wood surface as his hand fell onto the tabletop. He knew what was coming. I did not.

The judge said, "I find that the State has not presented any reliable evidence in this case. This case is hereby dismissed. Mr. Roybal you are free to leave."

Shock splintered the courtroom like a strong volt of electricity fingers its way across a stormy sky. I held my breath while others gasped and cried behind me—both happy and tormented tears. I cried a little too after seeing the relief and water in Max's eyes. Terry looked at me and smiled. I turned and looked at Anne. She was crying, and had her arm around Max's daughter as she cried with her hands covering her pretty face.

Attorney Gore appeared to be experiencing a state of shock and an extreme sense of victory at the same time. Her eyes were wide in amazement. I gave Max a pat on the back. He thanked us and ran over to hold his daughter. Max had spent almost three years in jail awaiting trials on two murders charges, and now he was free, just like that. There simply was no reliable evidence to support the prosecution of Max Roybal.

After the press questioned defense attorney Terry, they came to me. I was still so flustered, I spouted out: "I'm ecstatic to see justice done. I knew it would go this way from the start." That was a stupid thing to say. Terry later counseled me, giving me a quick lesson in showing humility when talking to the media.

It was a short walk to the hotel next door where we planned to stay for the duration of the trial. We sat in the lounge; all of us taking turns saying, "Holy shit!" Guess we didn't need to book rooms after all.

Laura's mother, who so kindly and softly accepted my

words of condolence just hours before in the women's room, entered through the oversized glass reception doors. She was looking down at the marble tile floor as if she lost something very valuable. Her face was ashen, stressed, and more tormented than before. She looked over and stabbed me intently with piercing icy shards from her eyes. Direct hit.

I do not think my heart could have sunk any deeper into the hotel lobby's leather sofa. I have never felt so right and so wrong at the same time. My mind was jumping out of my seat and running over to Ms. Cecere, spouting everything I knew about the case, especially what I'd uncovered about Devilia. But tethered to my ankles were the ball and chain of legal propriety. I stayed glued to my seat, wiped the smile from my face, and gave another half-smile of condolence. This time she was not receptive.

Ms. Cecere's painful walk across that lobby still crushes me to this day. She didn't look at anyone else but me, not even Terry. I closed the file and tried to put it behind me.

I asked Terry why the police dropped the investigation merely because Max was found not guilty. Do they just think the judge got it wrong? They don't come ask me what I uncovered? They don't keep looking for her killer? "This system is messed up," I ranted.

Don't forget that we didn't have an opportunity to publicly expose all the investigation on alternate suspects. No one knew about my interviews and research of others who might have harmed Laura.

It's the job of the defense investigator to find evidence to impeach as many prosecution witnesses as possible, find alternate suspects, blow holes in prosecution's forensic theories, and, of course, bring to light any witnesses and physical evidence that support the innocence of the defendant. The defense attorney then sifts through all I bring to the table for him or her to use. Then he or she decides what evidence is compelling, relevant, and in what manner to present it in court.

It is also the attorney's job to deliver the evidence in an understandable and passionate manner before the triers of fact (the jury), at which phase the defense investigator takes a back seat unless needed to testify.

Mr. Terry permitted me to sit at the counsel table and assist him in this media-driven homicide case. In my two most recent homicide cases in Nevada, the judge would not allow me to sit in the courtrooms at all. Instead the prosecutor asked him to invoke the rule to exclude witnesses from the courtroom, meaning that anyone that might testify, even licensed professionals such as myself, are not allowed to listen to the ongoing trial.

No one asked me to leave the courtroom in Tennessee. It was the first and last time I have ever been interviewed by the media. A brief moment of recognition. Now back to the shadows I go.

One thing I didn't mention earlier after interviewing Devilia. There was some writing found on a bathroom wall at the military base. Base personnel believed it was related to the death of Laura Cecere. Military police, however, disregarded it.

The etching showed inference to a jawbone and ended with these words: "I'm not the kind of dog to just leave you like that." I remember Devilia saying, "I'm not that kind of person . . ."

I wonder if Laura told Devilia it was over, to stop fantasizing and leave her alone. Or was Devilia being truthful about she and Laura having planned to commit suicide together? If so, then why and how did Laura's jawbone show up at the local TV station?! Chilling.

Again, the jury never heard our case, nor did Ms. Cecere.

CASES IN THE NEWS
Michael Morton

Michael Morton's wife Christine was attacked and killed at their home in Williamson County, Texas. Morton was at work at the time. Still, authorities suspected him and charged him with the murders.

"Innocent people think that if you just tell the truth then you've got nothing to fear from the police," Morton says. "If you just stick to it that the system will work, it'll all come to light, everything will be fine." Not true.

Morton argued that there was no scientific evidence, no eyewitness, no murder weapon, and no believable motive. But with a passionate, tearful district attorney's presentation of his theory that Morton murdered his family because his wife was too tired to have sex that night, and with no other suspects, the jury convicted him. "We all felt so strongly that this was justice for Christine and that we were doing the right thing," said the jury foreman.

A group of pro bono (free) attorneys finally convinced the court that not only was Morton innocent, but the prosecutor withheld crucial evidence. The court agreed and Morton was released after almost 25 years in prison. [7]

Telling the Truth: Witnesses

Aside from favorable forensics and provable facts in a case, witnesses have the most influence upon a jury. Most of the cases I have investigated turned in favor of the defense based on a single witness that I was able to either impeach or from whom I learned important new information that was not divulged to the prosecution during their investigation.

In the Laura Cecere case, being able to impeach Susan Craft was key. In the Karen Anderson case, interviewing the cop and putting him on the stand helped convince the jury that Max Roybal did not murder her. One witness can easily make or break a case. This is why I consider witness-interviewing skills to be a top priority for investigators.

Not only does the investigator need to be able to gain the attention and trust of a witness, but the investigator must also be diligent in acquiring the interview.

I investigated a case in which our client, Mr. Y., shot and killed a young man who threatened him in a parking lot. After I completed an in-depth social media and criminal history background on the victim and his three friends at the scene, I concluded that these were members of a motorcycle gang with violent histories.

I was able to talk with one of the victim's friends several times, and he contributed very important information that the police forgot to turn over to the defense: they had drugs in the car that police confiscated, and the cop told them not to worry about it.

I interviewed the then-retired lead detective, who, basically, did no investigation on the case. He bragged about solving the case in the first six hours of his investigation and getting the victim and defendant scumbags off the street in one fell swoop.

He was unaware that I was recording our conversation. He said he couldn't care less about this case since he was now retired. It was fine with him if our client was charged with jaywalking at this point, but that he could make any case appear the way he wanted. He boasted, "I can make any case a death penalty case." We called him to testify and played the tape.

Another witness was near the scene and saw what happened after shots were fired. This woman had already been questioned by police officers and their report simply indicated "heard shots but saw nothing." Not a helpful witness.

What exactly did she not hear and not see? When I asked her directly, she told me: "Two shots and a man down in the parking lot." Yes, exactly what the police reported. But, really, that's it? Where were the friends of the victim? She then said the man was down and that no one was next to him for a couple of minutes, until EMS arrived. Aha! The cops didn't ask that question.

We called her to testify.

The prosecution said our client shot an unarmed man, yet we claimed self-defense. Defense counsel could now argue numerous points: 1) that police failed to investigate, 2) that the victim was a felon, and, 3) that the victim's friends were ex-felons getting rid of weapons at the time this woman saw the victim alone on the ground.

If your friend had just been shot, wouldn't you be right there with him? We argued that it was a justifiable homicide: shooting and killing the victim in self-defense. We won a full acquittal for our client Mr. Y.

Ideally all witnesses should be neutral and unbiased, but they aren't. My job is to find witnesses who help make a case for innocence. My job is to vet the prosecution's witnesses. That means I investigate their credibility and whether or not their prior statements were reported accurately.

I'm always thrilled to befriend a prosecution witness that really doesn't like the prosecution's arguments in the case, or doesn't realize the prosecution is basing the case on his or her testimony. I'll interview such a witness more than once, if possible.

Witnesses do not want to be witnesses. I understand that. I want them to feel free to tell me everything, level with me, and trust me. I try to make witnesses feel important—they are important—and proud to stand up for the truth.

In many cases, these once-reluctant witnesses later evolve into persons full of pride and righteousness for coming forward and doing the right thing by testifying in court on behalf of justice. My approach is to impress upon the witness that he or she is not testifying in support of the defendant, but in support of the truth. The witness is only there to tell us what he or she observed, and not to take sides.

In another case, prosecutors charged our client, Mr. Z. with first-degree murder for shooting two transients in his vacant family home, killing one of them.

The prosecution's theory was that the transients were asleep after injecting methamphetamine into their veins two hours prior. (Really?!! Surely you jest Mr. Prosecutor! Meth is a drug that awakens the user. It's speed.) Then supposedly as they slept, the defendant opened fire on them without cause. The prosecution needed to prove that the defendant shot and killed an innocent, unaggressive person.

Mr. Z. agreed to be interviewed by police immediately following the shooting. During his interview he was clearly confused and in shock, and made errors relating to the details of the shooting. Of course, the prosecution used this against him in trial by suggesting Mr. Z. could not keep his facts straight because he was lying.

While it is standard law enforcement procedure for an officer who just shot and killed someone to immediately go on 48-hour paid leave with counseling before speaking with internal affairs investigators, citizens having experienced the same type of event are expected to immediately tell their whole story in detail to police interrogators. If they do not, then prosecutors can and do use that fact against the client at trial by saying they were uncooperative and further implying that this means they're guilty.

No one has to speak to police after an incident, nor should they be pressured to do so immediately following an incident.

I, personally, would rather be characterized by police as uncooperative than to offer them a statement of innocence that they twist and contort into evidence of guilt. I recently discussed this with a friend who is an ex-cop and current firearms instructor. He commented, "Cops write down what they THINK they heard you say!" Once it's in a police report, it's an uphill battle to overcome their account of your statement (unless, of course, it was recorded).

In Mr. Z.'s case, I interviewed the only partial eyewitness—an eyewitness being someone who actually sees something first-hand.

This man was present in the driveway when Mr. Z. entered the residence, and was also standing outside the front door when shots were fired inside the residence. He was an important witness in support of the prosecutor's argument that Mr. Z. was the aggressor. This is a crucial distinction because a person who kills another in self-defense can never be the initial aggressor. The police incident report indicated that this eyewitness stated that Mr. Z. was moving hastily and with determination, and the prosecutor decided this meant Mr. Z. was being aggressive.

This man told me a different story, and when we talked about his police interview, he said police had misquoted him. He said the defendant was pale, appeared to be in shock after firing his weapons, and told him that the people inside pointed a gun at him. While he was on the stand at the trial, the prosecutor accused this witness of altering his story and that I, perhaps, influenced him. Not true. The witness himself was disgusted with police tactics and the prosecutor's lethargy in following up with his requests to correct the record before trial.

From my perspective, this was a good and honest man who cared about accurately relating the details of what he observed.

I also interviewed a percipient witness (a person who has information but is not an actual eyewitness) who police reported as having seen the defendant investigating a break-in at the same property with a gun in hand a week prior to the shooting incident. The police report indicated she was very concerned that someone was going to get hurt. She was yet another potential important prosecution witness.

When I interviewed this woman, she intimated that police took her statement out of context. In fact, she was afraid that the defendant, a nice older man, was going to be hurt by transient burglars at some point because police were not responding to repeated calls to investigate the ongoing situation, and residents had to take matters of investigation into their own hands.

The prosecutor was blindsided because he had not followed up or comprehensively interviewed his own witnesses. In this case, two of the prosecution's presumed "star" witnesses ended up having more to say in support of the defense than the prosecution.

Significantly, the police did not thoroughly canvass the neighborhood to learn about additional witnesses. I was also able to find a homeless person who was a great witness, impeaching the testimony of the surviving victim, which proved to be very important.

For me, talking to witnesses is an exercise in both courage and authenticity. Basically I'm a shy person. A very quiet person. My parents expected young children to be respectful, quiet, and take a back seat to adults. I learned at a young age to keep my mouth shut, watch, and listen—good training for a private investigation career.

Before a witness interview I have to spend time getting mentally ready, psyching myself up. I dread cold-calling witnesses: showing up unannounced, unexpected, and unwelcome.

My parents taught me to always do a good job and take pride in my work and myself. That is a work ethic I agree with and have stood by in all my endeavors. When I clean a toilet, it's clean. Likewise, when I have to cold-call a witness, I do so with gusto. You would never know that behind my confident investigator facade, I'm a shy little girl who would rather be home writing books. The thing is, you have to live something before you can write about it.

I find it simpler, easier, and more empowering to be authentic . . . all politics aside. I think people can sense that I'm a "real" person. I don't shy away from allowing my personality to shine through or revealing personal information to witnesses (and clients). So what? We're all just people making our way through life. I've had much success getting people to talk candidly, so clearly this practice works . . . for me.

I will never just leave a business card and expect someone to call me for an interview. I will knock, and knock, and knock, waiting until the witness comes home, without being a bother. They don't know I've been there six times before finding them at home. They don't know I've waited in my car for several hours. It's the only way to get good results.

Occasionally, a witness will be outright rude to me. I'm the bad guy because I work for the defense, "the dark side."

Someone murdered the witness's friend, and I'm trying to help the person that the media or the cops told them did it. I get it.

The defense has an unpopular reputation, but there is no rational basis for this misperception of defense professionals. Though I do understand how extremists—staunch crusaders who not only voice their opinions but instigate confrontations and advance hate talk—can cause people to stereotype all defense professionals as rebellious, murderer-loving idealists. As in any case, stereotypes are not very representative of a population.

Most people don't stop to consider the many ways defense teams are protecting them—and even protecting the victim. Think about it: if police got the wrong guy, then I'm helping not only to free an innocent person but to bring awareness that justice has not yet been served on behalf of the victim . . . the bad guy is still out there.

Just like checks and balances in our government, defense teams are necessary to maintain balance in the justice system. Too many innocent people are arrested. Certainly you might agree that each case should be investigated by the defense to help avoid wrongful convictions. Many people don't understand the good we're doing—not just for our clients, but for the public as well.

Some folks are extremely closed off to hearing anything other than what they've already concluded in their minds. Of course, they don't even know all the facts of the case. They only know what the police said or what a TV reporter read from a teleprompter.

It's like watching the O.J. Simpson trial on TV and believing you know the answer, for a fact. Not even the jury in a trial hears all of the actual evidence. Imagine how much is left out of the media's presentation.

I literally did haul ass out of a house once for fear that I would be harmed. Although I already informed this elderly couple that I worked for the defense before they invited me inside their home, in the middle of the interview their adult son asked me again whom I represented. These nice people became very angry in a short second.

I'd never seen anything like it. The young bull came at me as if I was waving a red cape and I RAN out of there! I have never understood why people don't want to hear and question all of the evidence before convicting someone. They are driven purely by negative emotion, which is not helpful to anyone.

Experts, like laypersons, are called as witnesses, except they're skilled in a particular field of knowledge that is relevant to the issues in the case. I challenge their opinions in my interviews, and they often say I'm right. How can that be, you ask?

This isn't the effect of them being mistaken or me knowing more than they do. They tell me I'm right because sometimes the prosecutor didn't ask them the questions I ask. The prosecutor only asked a narrow set of questions, which they answered. The prosecutor didn't ask if there were other possible options or conclusions.

This proved to be a major issue in Hope Schreiner's post-conviction ineffective assistance of counsel appeal, which I investigated after she'd been convicted of second-degree murder. In her case, the prosecution presented an expert in the field of toxicology in order to pin down the time of death. The time range had to be very narrow because the defendant had an alibi for the rest of the day.

The prosecution asked the toxicologist if a particular scenario, which they provided to the toxicologist, was possible. He acknowledged that indeed it was possible. The questioning ended and the judge excused the witness.

Hope Schreiner's inexperienced defense counsel, who had never tried a murder case, didn't know that time of death could not be determined based on toxicology in that case, and that it was only one possible scenario among hundreds of possible scenarios. These are tricks prosecutors play with people's lives.

The defense attorneys did not make the effort to consult with a toxicology expert of their own in order to learn about the fallibility of the state expert's direct examination. (Direct examination is when the prosecutor and defense counsel question their own witnesses on the stand in a trial. After direct examination, the other side poses cross-examination questions to the same witness in an attempt to bring to light fallacies, misstatements, and evidence that might support that side's argument.)

Hope's defense attorneys likely didn't even consider the necessity of this effort, being inexperienced in defending a serious criminal charge. More on this case later.

I like to know the facts. I like to question the experts because even if they don't tell me what I want to hear, at least I know where they stand. I also learn more about the topic for my own forensics education, and now and then I discover that their testimony, when given comprehensively, actually supports the defense. I think many defense teams steer clear of prosecution witnesses, and I've learned that is a huge mistake.

Although experts are supposed to be neutral and unbiased, those that are on salary with the government often work together with police. What this typically means is that they don't actually investigate and comprehensively test all the characteristics of the forensic evidence. Instead, they only perform an individual test requested by police, and worse, they are asked by police to look for something specific and to only answer that narrow question—leaving available additional information unreported.

For example, when the police collect a fired bullet at an incident scene, they often take it to "their" lab and request the fingerprint examiner to check for the defendant's fingerprints on the bullet. That's it.

They do not ask whose fingerprint is on the bullet if not the defendant's. They do not necessarily preserve the fingerprint if it is not the defendant's print. They do not ask the examiner to determine whose blood, if any, is on the bullet. They do not ask if there are fibers on the bullet, and what they came from. They only want to know if the defendant loaded the bullet into his gun, and that is all the examiner looks for. Then the bullet is cleaned and placed back into evidence storage.

Once the bullet is cleaned, of course, unless the expert holds onto a forensic sample, all probative value for blood, DNA, fingerprints, and fibers is lost and the defendant has no recourse to obtain that information.

I recently read a case document in which a detective literally stated on his examination request: "We're looking for anything connecting the defendant to this evidence." That was it. The police were apparently not interested in knowing who was connected to the evidence, only whether the defendant was tied to it. Shameful.

I'm not saying every police detective works in this fashion, but one forensic examiner in a county lab told me that this is the way it often goes down. They only provide results per the request.

In effect, police officers are the prosecutor's investigators, although they are supposed to be neutral. Cops are in place to ensure the welfare of the people, not the prosecution of the people. However, cops are more typically working from a perspective of guilt, and I must work to check their math, so to speak. When they are clearly biased, as happens from time to time, it actually makes my job easier. In those cases we can point out their bias to the jury, as well as any mistakes they made due to inadequate investigation.

Unfortunately, too often, the bias is not clear and the jury will believe the prejudiced cop or the expert's narrow report, unless defense investigates and gets hold of the bigger picture to present to the jury.

Prosecutors have their own in-house district attorney office investigators, but they still know they need cops on their side. Police officers are supposed to be objective truth seekers. They're supposed to be protecting all of us from harm. That would include protecting us from malicious prosecution.

One might suggest that a defense investigator could be biased as well. Fair enough. For me, there is simply NO WAY I'm going to falsify a report on behalf of any person charged with crime. Why in the world would I do that, risking my license and my career?

I don't just assume a client is innocent merely because I

work for defense. If he's guilty, then so be it. I still need to help represent him and find evidence to support defense—which could mean evidence that supports a plea deal or lesser sentence. If defense teams did not do this, then police could arrest whoever they wanted and no one would look into it.

When I see someone in handcuffs, I admit there's a little voice in my head asking: "Oooh, wonder what he did!" I have to shake that inclination off and get back to the reality that a lot of innocent people are handcuffed. The more work I do as a defense investigator, the more that voice is rightly quieted.

Am I going to tell you a client is guilty? No. Not only is that privileged information (confidential attorney-client information), but that would also be counter-productive to my duties to support the defense. Besides, clients do not usually tell me they are guilty.

I am critical and suspicious by nature. Just ask my mother. She says that starting around the age of one or two I didn't let strangers near me. I would hold her hand and hide behind her leg.

I began opening up to people only after my mother went on a campaign to have everyone who came in contact with me pick me up and hug me. I now hug drug dealers and convicted murderers on a regular basis. In my professional experience, I've never met any Charlie Manson types. The folks I have met who were convicted of murder seem otherwise just like the average neighbor. If you had a conversation with one of them, you would never know they killed someone unless they told you.

People are people. I'm proud to be a compassionate person. We make mistakes, we're angry and misguided, and until we know better, we don't know any better.

I've found that understanding human frailty goes a long way. I do believe that if we perpetuate hate and condemnation, we will simply get more of it. Idealistic, I know. Still, it's my truth.

A better response might be to set the energy of awareness and positivity in motion, which means empowering everyone to be the best they can be instead of condemning them at their worst. Find what is right and expand that, which theoretically should then diminish what is energetically negative. Easy for me to say, I know. I feel you. I've seen the destruction and devastation created by twisted souls.

The difference between me and a cop is that many police officers will stop at the first or second sign of guilt and move on to the next case. They don't always follow through and validate the information. In most cases, they don't have the luxury of time to do this.

Unless you're caught in the act or there is good DNA evidence, actually, it's quite hard to prove guilt completely. Prosecution can surmise guilt. We know the prosecution has only to convince a jury of guilt beyond a reasonable doubt, not to actually prove it. Fewer people would end up in jail if prosecutors had to prove actual guilt.

Likewise, more people would be in jail if defense attorneys had to prove actual innocence. What are your thoughts on convicting someone based only on circumstantial evidence—with no physical evidence or reliable eyewitness? It happens every day. They tried to convict Max Roybal—twice.

Regardless of what I know or personally believe, my job is to poke holes in the prosecution's theory of guilt and work the case without a personal agenda. Of course, if my guy is most likely guilty, I still look for arguments and evidence to create reasonable doubt, but I'm never going to falsify my reports. I was once accused of falsifying a witness statement report by a small town prosecutor in Northern California. It really scared me because someone could lie about my actions and I could lose my license.

The witness I spoke with decided to change his mind (in order to protect himself from arrest) and told the prosecutor a different story than he told me. As I have stated, there is NO WAY IN THE WORLD I'm going to falsify a report.

Although I work for the defense, I still believe folks should pay for their crimes against society. In fact, I'd love to work cold cases for the government, in addition to my defense work.

This witness told me he initially made a false police report by telling police the defendant was guilty as charged, but, in fact, he later told me that the defendant was actually partially innocent. This witness reached out to us to help him correct the record.

After the defense attorney submitted my report to the prosecutor, the prosecutor threatened to arrest the witness for making a false report to a police officer. Subsequently, the witness then told the prosecutor that my report was made up.

Nowadays, when a witness makes a confession to me, I get it in writing if possible and take a photo of the witness holding his or her statement in front of their face. I made a mistake in that earlier case, and I own it. It was a big wake-up call for me professionally. It did occur to me to have the witness sign something, and I know he would have at the time. I'm not sure why I didn't ask him to, even though I got the pen out and it was in my hand. Instinctively, I knew I needed him to sign a formal statement. I failed the defendant in this case.

Witnesses, though they might appear to be very sincere, and actually are sincere at the time I speak with them, can simply change their minds. Or they can be coerced by the prosecution to cover up the truth. The prosecutor was not interested in the truth of the matter, just a full conviction, even if it was based on a lie.

Sometimes, I can uncover compelling evidence pointing toward innocence. If proof of innocence exists, then law enforcement should have known about it too. Remember, there's only one of me investigating a single case, and sometimes dozens of law enforcement tasked with investigating the same case. If I can find evidence of innocence, why can't they? Maybe they are not looking for it.

I have immense gratitude for citizens who put themselves out on the streets rounding up "bad guys" so that we can all be safer. I guarantee you, if I were a police offer I would be a good and honest one, and I would still make mistakes simply by virtue of various pressures and limited time. Therefore, while they have all the tools and resources at their disposal, maybe I have the greater advantage in terms of time and pacing.

Getting a great interview—meaning a candid and complete one—is a result of being personable, reasonable, and authentic, in my opinion. For me, it takes courage because it's not my nature to bother people. Getting a great interview can turn a case in favor of the defense in a heartbeat. It takes heart to do it: sincerity and stamina. This, I believe, is the most important task of a defense investigator.

While I say I dread walking up to a stranger and asking for that person's time and impressions on a criminal matter, I also love the interviews in which a witness is interested, forthcoming, and appreciative of my efforts. Then I can successfully mine the gold that lies beneath the surface of the criminal allegation against my client.

CASES IN THE NEWS
Brian Banks

Brian Banks was a student and star football player in high school, on the way to the big leagues with interest from UCLA and USC, when a fellow student accused him of rape. He accepted a plea deal to avoid a potential 41-year prison sentence and ended up serving five years. After his release, however, he was a jobless registered sex offender.

Wanetta Gibson's family had received a $1.5 million settlement from the school following Banks' guilty plea for failing to keep Wanetta safe.

Gibson, feeling guilty so many years later, sent Banks a Facebook message and agreed to meet him and a private investigator who recorded her confession of the false rape allegation against Banks.

Banks' attorneys also discovered that after the alleged rape, no male DNA had been detected on Gibson's underwear, and the classmate Gibson first told about the alleged attack said Gibson later admitted to making up the story so her mother wouldn't find out she was sexually active.

The case was finally dismissed after 10 years. "It's not our job to maintain a conviction at any cost," Deputy Dist. Atty. Brentford Ferreira said. "It's our job to do justice." He further stated that prosecutors had no plans to charge Gibson, saying it would be a difficult case to prove. [8]

Hope Schreiner: Defender Pretenders

Hope Schreiner

As I clicked through cable TV channels one day in 2006, I paused on the *Nancy Grace Show*. I intended to watch only for a moment and then move on. Nancy Grace wasn't my favorite commentator, but I found her to be entertaining. I only wanted to see which case she was passionate about that day. It was a lazy afternoon for me in beautiful Lake Tahoe.

Glancing out the window, I took in my treehouse view of woods, meadows, and Sierra Mountains. I was taking time off from investigation work in Tennessee, having just bought a second home in California.

Anne and I simply enjoyed life near the lake and the healthy environment. The water out of the faucets is completely drinkable! There seem to be millions more stars in the sky, fresh air, tranquil beauty and wildlife all around. I felt at home the instant I visited South Lake Tahoe.

During my sabbatical from investigation work, I did fun things like home renovations, and dealing and playing poker in town and on cruises around the world. All that, plus downhill and cross-country skiing in the winter, and motorcycle riding and hiking in the summer. What a life! Going back to "work" didn't seem all that interesting.

A photo inset of an older woman stared back at me from the lower left hand corner of the television screen. A caption flashed below the photo: "Hope Schreiner – Murder Defendant." Huh?

I knew a person named Hope Schreiner. She was a family friend when I was a child. I listened, as Grace summarized, "73-year-old librarian in Vermont accused of bludgeoning her husband to death in the driveway of their own home shows no emotion in her court trial." What? Vermont? That's where my childhood family friends live. I have not heard about them in years now.

I immediately felt as though I was about to come out of my semi-retirement. Within 30 seconds, I had phoned my mother. "Mom! Stop what you're doing and turn on the Nancy Grace show. Hope Schreiner is being tried for murdering Bob!"

"Are you sure it's Hope?"

"Yes, mom. Turn it on."

"Oh my goodness. I'll do it right now."

I hung up the phone and watched the half-hour commentary by Nancy Grace, who obviously despised Hope. Grace joked about the chief librarian and spouted something like, 'Death in the driveway, how could a granny do it?'

Grace was a prosecutor, so I guess her overexcitement and

eagerness to persecute a defendant reflected the way people expected her to act on the show. Although I'm certain Nancy Grace is a caring person (having seen her cry on her show), she appears insensitive to the plight of others, especially those accused of crimes. She often jokes about the demeanor or appearance of a defendant.

It's one thing for a defendant to be bashed on national television, but commentators don't seem to be sensitive to the fact that the defendants' families are likely watching. Or perhaps they just don't care.

Poor Hope. From where I was sitting, she looked confused and in shock the entire time.

I didn't subscribe to the Court TV channel, but my mother watched portions of the actual trial of her old friend. Clearly my mother was outraged at the way the judge's rulings seemed so biased in favor of the prosecution. She'd call me and ask, in a fit of disgust, "Can the judge say that? How can a judge be so dismissive like that in the middle of a trial? The judge treats Hope as if she's guilty already. Why don't her attorneys do anything?"

I could only respond that a good judge wouldn't act that way, and that maybe Hope's attorneys could appeal on that basis if she was convicted. During sentencing, judges sometimes offer their personal opinion regarding a defendant's guilt. Frankly, I agree this should not be allowed, but I think they do it to make clear why they are handing down harsh sentences. The judge in Hope Schreiner's case clearly did not like Hope and her "emotionless" manner. Apparently it's not how the judge would have reacted if she (the judge) were on trial for killing her husband. Then again, how would she know unless it happened to her?

In 2015, I reviewed a post-conviction homicide case in Nevada for a young woman serving life for murdering her husband. Before the trial, her public defender did little to no investigation on her behalf. The young woman was crucified.

She asked me to review the facts of her case and summarize what could have—and should have—been investigated on her behalf before trial. I reviewed this young woman's case. There were numerous parallels to Hope Schreiner's case. Both women were convicted without a proper defense, and both judges openly berated the newly convicted women.

A sentencing hearing is when the family of the victim pleads for a harsh sentence, the defendant's family supports their loved one, and the defendant sometimes talks about his or her personal feelings.

During the young woman's sentencing hearing the judge actually called her "evil" because she was convicted of killing her husband while he was sleeping and she showed "no emotion" during the trial (according to the judge). I'm sorry, but a judge is not an expert in how someone deals with stress.

Hope Schreiner collapsed when the jury foreman read aloud the words, "In the charge of second-degree murder, we find the defendant Guilty." The woman was a librarian and a gardener. She was married for over 40 years with nine kids. How do you prepare for being convicted of murdering a family member? What demeanor is a person supposed to sustain over the course of a two-week fiasco broadcast to the entire world on *Court TV* and *The Nancy Grace Show*?

To have shown "no emotion," I'm sure is not accurate.

Certainly that Hope collapsed suggests that she was experiencing some emotion. I read commentary published by Hope's granddaughter, in which she described seeing Hope in court as follows:

"In person, her eyes were glassy and lifeless; she moved slowly, as if she were sedated. As they led her into the small courtroom, she was not handcuffed. Someone said to her, 'Look, Jessie's here.'Feeling nervous, I smiled and waved. She smiled faintly at me and sat down with her lawyer. I wasn't even sure if she recognized me. In truth, I hardly recognized her: her affect, her manner, her body language were all unfamiliar." [9]

Sounds like shock or the effects of medication to me.

To all of the defense attorneys in the world:

Please hire a defense investigator in every important case, and make sure the investigator is a good one. Equally as important, make sure you know what you're doing before you take on a murder case. People's lives are in your hands. Do not assume the client is guilty without fully investigating the case. Consult experts even if you do not end up using them. Your job is to ensure that the U.S. Constitution is upheld by providing adequate representation for EVERY citizen you represent. Make it zealous representation. Justice will prevail and your resumé will reflect your efforts.

Beyond these fundamental necessities in representing a criminal defendant, the issue of whether or not an attorney believes in the client's innocence should not alter the attorney's efforts on his or her behalf.

Schreiner's two attorneys had apparently never tried a murder case, according to Hope. An attorney can be very caring and concerned about doing a good job without knowing how to do a good job—and perhaps not knowing that they don't know.

I called my Mom after the *Nancy Grace* episode ended. "Mom," I said, "GET ME ON HOPE'S CASE!"

It was too late, of course. Hope Schreiner had been convicted of second-degree murder. She changed attorneys before her sentencing. The new attorney did have homicide case experience and talked Hope into waiving the sentencing hearing and agreeing to a 17-year sentence, in lieu of the 20-year maximum. What? The woman is 74 years old. That is a long sentence for anyone, but that is a life sentence for her.

My mother wrote Hope a letter and told her what I did for a living. Hope knew she got a very raw deal at trial. She took the 17-year sentence because she thought the judge, who she felt hated her, would give her the maximum of 20 years. Hope didn't know I was a criminal defense investigator with experience in homicide defense. She was happy to hear from my mother.

Hope wrote me a letter from prison. Her post-conviction attorney didn't talk about using an investigator on her behalf, but Hope understood that she needed a good one. Therefore, she circumvented her attorney and hired me directly.

Every lawyer must try their first case, but it is essential to consult with an experienced co-counsel, or at least an advisor or mentor, when stepping up into new arenas. I do not begrudge Hope's attorneys for wanting to work a murder case and grow their brand, and I'm certain they made their best effort. Had I been their investigator pre-trial, I would have suggested they seek mentorship from learned counsel highly experienced in homicide defense.

According to the newspapers, one of the attorneys was going through a divorce at the time of the trial. This must have provided a major distraction for both attorneys during Hope's trial.

Hope's post-conviction attorney had a reasonable argument for getting a retrial due to the fact not enough was done for Hope at trial. Unfortunately, the court didn't grant a retrial. This was a terrible miscarriage of justice, in my opinion.

The trial attorneys did not put defense experts on the stand to refute the state experts' findings. They did minimal investigation. Moreover, the trial attorneys' cross-examination constantly reiterated and reinforced the prosecution's points.

The defense attorneys did not present an argument about forensics, and how the forensics related to the time of death. They did not investigate the concerns of their own client: that Hope was afraid of a local townsperson who she believed, in fact, murdered her husband. This man was never investigated by defense.

That said, the evidence presented by the prosecution did look bad for Hope, but it should have been investigated and refuted through experts and evidence, not merely through legal disagreement with the State's presentation. Hope's new attorney could only get her a new trial if he could prove that:

1. There was evidence of actual innocence—meaning proof that someone else did it; and/or,

2. New evidence had come to light that was not available at the time of trial, and such new evidence strongly supported

innocence, for example, if a stranger came forward with a solid alibi for the defendant, and a new DNA test showed the defendant was not a match; and/or

3. The defendant's trial attorneys were so inept that the trial was not fair.

The formal term for appealing the proficiency of trial counsel is an ineffective assistance of counsel (IAC) claim.

Ineffective assistance of counsel has a two-pronged standard. Not only does the petitioner (prior defendant) have to show the trial attorneys failed to represent him or her properly by not presenting important evidence pointing toward innocence, but the petitioner also must show that the evidence that could have been presented would have made a very meaningful difference in the outcome of the trial.

You must convince the new judge that trial counsel was deficient, and that such deficiency resulted in extreme prejudice that precluded the defendant from receiving a fair trial. Convincing the judge of this is very difficult in most cases. Often they will rule that an attorney's actions or omissions fall into the "trial strategy" category. No judge wants to overturn a conviction based on an ineffective assistance of counsel claim unless there were decisive, gross errors.

New evidence supporting innocence is rarely enough. As far as new evidence is concerned, someone would have to come forward and confess to the murder and have matching DNA. This would be an example of "actual innocence."

By way of an example, I investigated a capital post-conviction case many years ago in which the trial judge allowed 11 women and one man to sit as jurors to decide the fate of a man who beat and drowned his wife.

I went to the residence of this retired judge and questioned him. When I asked about the unusually high number of women on the jury, he said, "Well, honey, all the men had to work to support those women, so I let them off to work." Then he made what I considered a romantic advance. The man was in his 80s. This client admitted killing his wife, but I never felt it was premeditated first-degree murder. He was convicted and sentenced to death.

Convincing an appellate judge that trial attorneys were not up to par in any case is not easy. In the capital case with the 11 female jurors, the defense counsel later admitted he was using cocaine during portions of the trial and falling asleep during other portions. He also conducted no investigation, and allowed 11 women to sit on the jury.

They did not win on the inadequate attorney claim because the appeal judge believed the defendant still would have been found guilty regardless of his counsel's deficiencies. I'm not sure how a judge can make such a ruling without a full investigation of the case facts by the defense, which still had not been undertaken on the convicted's behalf. No investigation was done during the appeal stage either, and as a result, there was nothing new to present to the judge. The same was true in Schreiner's case . . . minimal pre-trial investigation and nothing further prior to direct appeal.

Read on and let me know what you think. Did Hope Schreiner get a fair trial? Could she have won her freedom with a competent defense team?

Hope Schreiner: Pharmaceuticals & Pink Toenails

I contacted the private investigation licensing board of Vermont and requested special permission to travel there to conduct a post-conviction investigation of this case. The licensing board granted me a 30-day permit, and I drove 17 hours from central Tennessee to Southern Vermont. My parents live in Vermont so I stayed with them, saving Ms. Schreiner money, and made the hour-and-a-half drive each day to the town where the murder took place to conduct witness interviews.

The Schreiner case was a made-for-TV circus of dramatic events. After 43 years of marriage, Hope was having an affair with a local widower. So when did that make someone a murderer?

She raised her kids from an abusive prior marriage, raised Bob's kids from his prior marriage, and then raised the child they had together. She kept the house clean and orderly. She kept the gardens.

Hope endured the traumatic murder of her own teenage daughter, Leslie, who was picked up hitchhiking by the wrong guy. Leslie Schreiner was my brother's age. They used to ski together. I remember this horrible turn of events when I was an adolescent.

Leslie was independent, athletic, outgoing, and full of life. She fought off the advances of the driver and he crashed the car, paralyzing her. She recounted the events before falling into a coma from which she never awoke. She was 15. I never hitchhiked again after Leslie Schreiner's death.

Hope volunteered at the local library, played tennis with the women at the local club, and now and then shared some moments of youth and vitality with her neighbor Paul.

Bob was neither interested nor able to provide romantic husbandly services to Hope. She and Bob were comfortable in their platonic marriage. The Schreiners' good friend Richard explained to me very clearly that Bob knew about the affair and was completely fine with it.

Of course, the kids didn't know about it, and some of them were angry with their mother when it came out at trial. After so many years of marriage, sometimes the romance fades and the partners simply become friends, taking care of one another. This is not atypical at all. Hope and Bob stayed together despite the fact that their romantic relationship was long over.

The prosecutor used the affair and the notion that Hope no longer wanted to care for her ailing husband as the motive for her killing Bob. Although Bob did suffer from serious health conditions including COPD, a limp, Hepatitis C, and a prior cancer diagnosis, he also went into town every day on his own, played poker with friends, volunteered on committees, and drove himself to New Hampshire for doctor visits. I'm not sure how much he relied on Hope for anything.

Bob told their good friend Richard that if Hope wasn't happy, he understood and would not stand in her way. She and Bob were already sleeping in separate quarters. The affair was simply not an issue of great importance.

Couldn't she just say, "I'm outta here"? After all those years, the marital money would have been divided equally no matter what.

From what I learned, Hope's romantic interludes with Paul occurred every now and then. Their affair was a casual thing. It wasn't serious. There were no plans to run away together. I spoke at length with Hope, Paul, and Richard on this issue. Of course, trial counsel didn't present what I found because they didn't investigate the issue before trial. Trial counsel did little to nothing to refute the affair as motive, or to refute the notion that Bob relied on Hope to take care of him as a motive.

Richard, who knew the Schreiners for years, also told me that Bob and Hope bickered just like any married couple, but had no animosity toward one another. This sentiment was supported by other friends of the couple as well. Richard often chuckled at the couple's verbal sparring bouts.

It was Draggon, a local townsman, who hated both Hope and Bob Schreiner. He was a man with emotional problems. Hope's defense attorneys completely dismissed her suspicions of Draggon as the real murderer and never investigated him.

I learned that Draggon lived alone. On multiple occasions, Richard witnessed Draggon screaming obscenities "at the top of his lungs" at the Schreiners, an elderly couple.

Bob had a sharp tongue and quite plainly told Draggon where he could go. According to Richard, Draggon was "off."

He also said that Hope openly feared Draggon both before and after Bob's murder.

Richard was the only known person, aside from Hope (and the victim), who was on their property on the morning of Bob's murder. Richard visited the Schreiners' house that day, but nobody answered his knock at the door.

Incredibly, neither Hope's defense attorneys nor their investigator privately questioned Richard prior to trial. Instead, Richard was only deposed jointly by the prosecutor and the defense counsel, as if it were a civil case.

According to Richard, they asked him useless questions at trial. They asked him nothing about the Schreiners' relationship, their dealings with Draggon, or the details of what Richard observed—and what he did not observe—in the driveway that morning.

Both Richard and his wife are confident, to this day, that Hope is innocent. They both characterize the trial as "a farce," as if her own attorneys never considered the possibility that she might be innocent.

Another neighbor agreed that the trial was a "complete joke." They commented to me that the prosecution put its case on for days, then the defense put its case on in approximately two hours. That was it. "They did absolutely nothing for Hope at trial," according to this neighbor.

As it turned out, none of the prosecution lay witnesses would speak with me. (A lay witness is an average, every day person, if you will . . . unlike an expert witness.) Two women, who were Hope's friends prior to the murder, had run to Hope's house when they noticed police cars and flashing lights. Later on they suspected that Hope killed Bob. They based their suspicions on the belief that, by their estimation, Hope exhibited "unusual" behavior after the murder.

A neighbor at the scene, Ms. Leaf, asked Hope what happened, and reported to police that Hope said she "just snapped." This statement is completely out of context, as there was no specific question and no reference to subject matter—only an assumption about the meaning of Hope's alleged comment. And, of course, the recollection might not even be accurate. Hope told me she didn't remember saying this—or anything else that was said at the incident—because she was distraught.

How does anyone know how another person will act in the face of such a stressful, horrible event? One of the women brought Hope to her home that night, offering her safety and companionship. In the middle of the night, this friend awoke and "recalled" that Hope had said earlier in the day, "Don't worry, I did it." She later told police of this remembrance . . . or was it a dream? According to Hope's daughter-in-law, this witness confided that police had pressured her to give them something against Hope.

Does it make sense to you to bring someone to your house who just confessed to killing her husband? How would you not recall such a confession?

You might be familiar with the phrase "hearsay evidence," and know it refers to something that someone heard from another person, and is not allowed in court. While that is true for the most part, there are exceptions to the Hearsay Rule. One exception is called Spontaneous Utterance. In this case, Hope allegedly spontaneously uttered "Don't worry . . . I did it," to her friend.

The fact that it was only recalled upon waking from sleep was not argued by Hope's defense attorneys. So was it a confession? If so, then it defies hearsay and is allowed in court. Or was it a dream? In that case it is not allowed in court. Regardless, the prosecution won over the jury with this alleged confession by Ms. Schreiner.

I spoke with the Schreiner's close friend Richard and his wife. I spoke to more friends, auto mechanics, and neighbors. I spoke to Draggon, who answered the door wearing pink toenail polish and quickly began ranting about hating Hope, and needing to take Ambien to sleep. He was curiously intense and scattered, yet keeping a lid on something about to blow . . . like the calm before a major storm.

I called Draggon a couple of hours later because I forgot to ask an important question. He immediately cursed me to hell and rampaged about how my in-person visit had severely upset him, triggering his PTSD and causing him to suffer an intense emotional setback; he was in therapy; he ran away from his hometown in order to "escape" a childhood trauma; and he went on in what seemed like a single psycho sentence.

He scared me! He was friggin' off the wall!! I'm so glad I wasn't face-to-face with him during this conversation because I would have been afraid he would become violent. He was spitting mad, and I held the phone back from my ear as if his acidic saliva would come through the receiver and eat the flesh off my bones. Even holding the phone an arm's length away, I could still clearly hear each word he screamed at me.

The state's expert toxicologist testified at trial that he determined Bob's time of death based on the amount of sleeping medication Bob ingested the morning of his death.

Ambien! Yes, Hope and Bob both took Ambien for sleep. Apparently, so did Draggon. As presented by the prosecution's expert, the details of the murder unfolded like this: Hope laced Bob's morning coffee with seven 10-milligram pills of Ambien, went off to play tennis and run errands, and expected him to be dead when she returned home.

According to the prosecution, things did not go as Hope planned. She found Bob alive and well, just getting into his truck to go somewhere, and she beat him over the head with a potato hoe, which is a three-pronged metal rake. Bob had black eyes and multiple bruises on his face, in addition to lacerations and punctures in his head.

Throughout the investigation and trial, Hope's story never changed. Hope always stated she came home around 12:30 p.m. and walked the dogs—going in the other direction without seeing Bob in the remote corner of the driveway.

When she returned she saw him lying there. A retired nurse, Hope immediately called 911 and gave Bob CPR, knowing that Bob was inflicted with Hepatitis C. This was at around 1:40 p.m.

Emergency medical services arrived around 2:00 p.m. and pronounced her husband dead at the scene, estimating that he had been dead for two to three hours. EMS noted observing blood on Hope's hands and around her mouth, and no blood on her clothing.

Hope had a solid alibi for the two to three hours prior to EMS's pronouncement. Just before coming home, she went to the bank; her deposit slip was time stamped 12:21 p.m. This blew major holes in the prosecution's theory that Hope had drugged Bob at eight o'clock in the morning.

This did not present a problem for the prosecutors however. Why not? Because they revised the time of death.

The medical examiner—a state employee—who had already stated he typically relied on EMS's judgment of time of death, later expanded the range for time of death in his official report to be between 8:00 a.m. and 12:30 p.m—in other words, between the time Hope left and the time she returned home.

Hope's attorneys did not present defense experts to refute the time of death, or present defense experts to refute the state's "new" theory.

At trial, the prosecution used its toxicologist to determine a narrower time of death based on the amount of Zolpidem (Ambien) found in Bob's body. The new time of death? Just after Hope returned home.

Again, the defense attorneys offered no argument at all.

Remember the potato hoe? Gaylyn, Hope and Bob's daughter-in-law, borrowed the hoe after Bob's murder. First, Hope didn't hide the assumed murder weapon! Second, Gaylyn said it was antique, and as soon as she used it in the garden, it broke into pieces. I doubt that it could have been used to bludgeon a man to death. Gaylyn shared this information with Hope's attorneys and the police, but it apparently fell on deaf ears.

Hope Schreiner: Delaying Death

After my fieldwork investigation in Vermont, I returned home and immediately began researching the toxicology of Zolpidem. I'm a college business major and not at all versed in chemistry, but this was really an exercise in common sense.

I researched the time required for Zolpidem to fall to half its initial value (half-life). If 70 milligrams (7 pills) of Zolpidem were ingested at 8:00 a.m., according to the prosecution's theory, then how long until 55mg remained in the body? (I don't remember the exact amount now). Two hours? Four hours?

It appeared that the prosecution's expert started backwards, the same way I did, to determine how much and when something had been ingested. Start with what was in the body, then determine the half-life, and then come to a conclusion.

Regarding the time of death, the EMS stated two to three hours, and the medical examiner initially stated he relied on EMS judgment, but he later stated four to eight hours.

Thus, the prosecution simply asked the toxicologist this: if Bob had ingested seven 10mg Ambien at 8:00 a.m., would that be consistent with a time of death of 12:30 p.m. or soon thereafter? This was the very time Hope returned home.

He testified, "Yes."

Basically, that was the only question asked of him. Well, of course it was consistent, since we do not know the exact parameters of what we're talking about.

It occurred to me that the levels of Zolpidem in Bob's body at the time of death could be the result of more than one scenario. Wouldn't it also be consistent with taking 20mg of Ambien at 10:00 a.m.? This would certainly explain why Bob didn't answer the door when Richard came by the house between 10:30 and 11:00 a.m..

Richard parked in the driveway and didn't see any dead bodies. Couldn't the defense attorneys have used this witness to narrow down the time of the murder? Death did not occur before 10:30 a.m.

The State's toxicologist expert, Dr. Evans, ran a laboratory in Indiana. I drove to Indiana and asked him my question in person. He again said, "Yes," to me.

He agreed that the levels present in Bob's body could have also meant that he took 20mg of Ambien at 10:00 a.m., or countless other scenarios. No one could possibly conclude the time of death based on the amount of Ambien found in Bob's body.

Why didn't defense counsel ask this simple question at trial? State's expert Evans told me he was shocked that they hadn't asked.

I also spoke with two other expert toxicologists who could have been called on behalf of the defense who reconfirmed the same thing: "Time of death cannot be concluded from any toxicology in this case."

It's like trying to calculate a bullet trajectory with only one entry defect . . . you also need the exit defect to line up the trajectory path. Given only one level of drug in the blood at one time cannot provide an answer to when and how much was ingested.

Regarding EMS and medical examiners determining time of death, EMS said 11:00 a.m. to 12:00 p.m., meaning two to three hours before 2:00 p.m., when they pronounced Bob dead. And the medical examiner did rely on their observations, though he later changed his conclusions to fit the prosecution's theory.

One might ask why didn't the medical examiner take Bob's internal temperature when he arrived at the murder scene? Good question. He said he does not normally do that.

When EMS arrived at the scene, rigor mortis had set into the jaw only. Although air temperature causes somewhat varied results, typically this occurs after a couple of hours, again putting time of death around 12:00 p.m. Full rigor can set in anywhere from six to 12 hours after death, so once again, Bob's death was definitely not likely to have occurred at 8:00 a.m.

These are easy arguments for defense counsel to have introduced at trial. Hope's tennis friends also reported that she seemed perfectly normal, and nothing appeared to distract her.

Here is the affidavit of my findings and conclusions that I composed on Hope's behalf. It sets out the relevant evidence I uncovered and how that evidence would have been helpful at trial. Below is the full content [with some information and names changed or redacted] of my actual document that I presented to Hope's post-conviction attorney in an effort to get a new trial based on ineffective assistance of counsel:

STATE OF VERMONT **SUPERIOR COURT**
WINDHAM COUNTY, SS. **CIVIL ACTION**

In re: Hope Schreiner Docket No. ________

AFFIDAVIT OF APRIL HIGUERA

April Higuera, being of lawful age, states the following:

I am a licensed private investigator in the states of California and Tennessee. I was hired by Ms. Schreiner, the petitioner, through her attorney Jesse Conrad, to assist in the post-conviction investigation of her second-degree homicide charge. I was granted temporary permission from the state of Vermont's private investigation regulatory commission to enter the state and conduct a physical investigation, during which time, I met with Ms. Schreiner and also with several witnesses.

While I am aware of Strickland v. Washington and its two-pronged test for ineffective assistance of counsel, it is also my understanding and experience that judgment of inadequate representation is somewhat subjective in that different judges have defined their own standards for adequate assistance of counsel and, additionally, that if one issue of inadequacy does not meet the level for success on an IAC claim, then the cumulative impact of smaller inadequacies may reach the level of inadequate representation tipping the scales in favor of a new and fair trial for the petitioner, especially considering the gravity of the charge of homicide.

This affidavit includes some of my investigative findings and my expert opinion that trial counsel Wood and Bark failed to adequately investigate on behalf of Ms. Schreiner. In fact, it is my strong contention that the outcome of the trial would have been considerably more favorable to Ms. Schreiner, including possible acquittal, had a proper investigation been conducted pre-trial and presented to the jury in a comprehensive and understandable manner by experienced and undistracted attorneys.

My expert opinion that trial attorneys Wood and Bark failed to adequately investigate and perform at trial on behalf of Ms. Schreiner is outlined immediately below and supported further below:

a. failure to consult with defense experts
b. failure to investigate alternate suspects
c. failure to interview witnesses for defense
d. failure to consult with and inform client
e. lack of professional experience and personal attention to the case

BACKGROUND

Ms. Schreiner, a 71-year-old woman at the time, was accused, and later convicted, of bludgeoning her husband to death in broad daylight before either she left to play tennis and run errands at 8:30am, or when she arrived home after 12:30pm on June 2, 2004. The State theorized, and their experts supported, that Ms. Schreiner must have put seven 10mg Ambien prescription pills in the decedent's coffee around 8am, unbeknownst to him, and later beat him to death at 12:30pm or shortly thereafter. Defense counsel offered no experts of their own to either assist in their investigation or refute state experts at trial.

Had I been the defense investigator working with defense counsel Wood and Bark in the representation of Ms. Schreiner at trial, I would have contacted and interviewed numerous experts, including serologists, medical examiners, crime scene analysts, DNA analysts, and toxicologists in this case. No such expert assisted defense at trial. In my post-conviction investigation, I was able to determine through the experts that

I contacted, that the state's theory of time of death was not viable nor reasonable nor based on scientific facts or accurate testimony.

LACK OF INVESTIGATON – Experts

TIME OF DEATH – Toxicologist as defense expert

State expert toxicologist Michael Evans testified that the level of Zolpidem (Ambien) in the decedent's blood at the time of death was consistent with the theory that the decedent ingested seven 10mg Ambien pills with his coffee around 8am (just before Ms. Schreiner left to play tennis). Prosecution used this expert, alone, to suggest an actual time of death between 11:00am and 12:30pm. (The outer edge of Ms. Schreiner's alibi, as she was not on the scene of the crime between 8:30am until just after 12:30pm.) Prosecution disregarded the statements of EMS and other professionals on the scene who suggested an earlier time of death. Defense counsel was not effective in their cross-examinations nor did they offer experts to refute prosecution's time of death theory.

Had I been the defense investigator pre-trial, I would have interviewed Mr. Evans and another toxicologist on behalf of Ms. Schreiner. My post-conviction investigation clearly refutes prosecution's theory of time of death, and further places time of death during the hours in which Ms. Schreiner has a solid alibi.

I interviewed State's expert Michael Evans in 2008. Dr. Evans told me that there are literally hundreds of scenarios as to why and how the Zolpidem was in the decedent's blood and that prosecution only asked him if this one scenario was possible. He further told me that time of death cannot be determined based on the toxicology in this case. Dr. Evans specifically stated, "There is absolutely no way time of death can be determined in this case based on toxicology." This witness further informed me of his surprise that he was not deposed by defense pre-trial, nor adequately cross-examined at trial, nor did a defense toxicologist testify at trial on behalf of Ms. Schreiner.

I interviewed University of Tennessee's Glenn Farr, Pharm. Ph.D., and Professor of Clinical Pharmacy, who also stated there were literally hundreds of viable scenarios as to how and why the Zolpidem was in the decedent's system at the time of death, and that toxicology cannot be used to determine time of death in this case. Dr. Farr stated, "With just one toxicology drug level, it is absolutely impossible to determine the time of death or the time and amount of zolpidem consumed in this case."

I interviewed Vanderbilt University's Toxicologist Saralyn Williams, M.D. who informed me that Dr. Evan's calculations of the half-life of zolpidem (i.e., how long it takes the body to eliminate the drug) was most likely miscalculated because the decedent's age and liver disease were not taken into consideration. She said the half-life would likely be shorter. She also stated, as did Evans and Farr, that since only one post-mortem level of the Zolpidem is available, time of death cannot be determined by toxicology in this case.

Had Drs. Farr and Williams testified at trial on behalf of Ms. Schreiner, they would have refuted statements by Dr. Evans which prosecution used to tell the jury that time of death occurred just after Ms. Schreiner arrived home around 12:30pm. Furthermore, had defense simply deposed and adequately cross-examined Dr. Evans, the state's own expert, he, himself, would have told the jury that no time of death can be determined by the toxicology in the case, contrary to prosecution's theory.

TIME OF DEATH – Medical examiner as defense expert

Defense counsel did not put a defense expert on the stand at trial to explain or refute suggested time of death indicators promoted by state medical examiner experts Steven Shapiro, M.D. and Steven Shafer, M.D. Dr. Shafer arrived on the crime scene at 4:20pm and theorized, at that time, decedent had been "dead several hours." Later, after speaking with Ms. Schreiner and police, he revised and theorized that time of death had occurred some 4-8 hours earlier (8:20am-12:20pm – Ms. Schreiner has an alibi from 8:30am until just after 12:30pm). EMS on the scene at 1:50pm indicated time of death occurred two to three hours earlier (10:50-11:50am – Ms. Schreiner had an alibi during this time period).

Medical examiner Steven Shapiro, M.D., who performed the autopsy the following day, stated in his trial testimony that he usually relies on EMS for an accurate determination of time of death, as they are first on the scene, and although they are not considered time of death experts, they have considerable experience in determining such. Shapiro, however, indicated a time of death after 9:20am and later revised time of death to have occurred between 8:00am and 2:00pm, based on the statements of Ms. Schreiner as to when she last saw her husband alive at 8:00am and when EMS pronounced him dead at 2:00pm [1:50pm]. Prosecution prevailed in presenting their theory at trial that time of death occurred at approximately 12:30pm or just thereafter, based on the toxicology. Neither EMS nor the medical examiner on the scene agree with prosecution, but defense counsel did not present a theory of their own, nor effectively cross-examine state's experts at trial.

Had I been the defense investigator on this case pre-trial, I would have consulted with an expert medical examiner to assist in Ms. Schreiner's defense.

I interviewed medical examiner expert Howard Adelman, M.D. in 2008 who, based on the trial testimony, state medical examiner reports, photos, and other relevant testimony, determined time of death in this case to likely have occurred approximately three hours before decedent was found by Ms. Schreiner or EMS arrived on the scene (9:45-11:45am). Ms.

Schreiner has an established alibi during this time, accepted by prosecution. Dr. Ademan's theory of time of death is consistent with both the EMS and the state medical examiner's observations of the deceased on scene.

From my own research and experience, I have learned that rigor mortis usually onsets within two hours, first affecting the jaw and similar smaller muscles, while full rigor usually occurs within 6-12 hours of death [*DiMaio & Dana, Forensic Pathology*]. EMS observations of the deceased upon arrival at the scene in this case indicate rigor only in the jaw. EMS also indicated corneal cloudiness was present. My research indicates the earliest this condition usually occurs is two to three hours after death [*DiMaio & DiMaio*, *Forensic Pathology 2d*]. My research is consistent with the EMS and the medical examiner's observations and post-conviction defense medical examiner expert Dr. Adeleman's theory of time of death, not at all with the prosecution's theory presented at trial.

LACK OF INVESTIGATION – Alternate Suspects

Paul Driftwood – as a defense alternate suspect

Mr. Driftwood was having an affair with Ms. Schreiner at the time of her husband's death. He left town the day after the body was found, and he later lied to police that he had not been intimate with decedent's wife at any time. ████████ ████████████████. He has no alibi the day of the homicide. Mr. Driftwood has never, to this day, been thoroughly investigated, but even so, could have been offered to raise a cumulative rationale of reasonable doubt.

████████ – as a defense alternate suspect

Mr. █████ was identified by an inmate in the New Hampshire correction system, during the trial, as the murderer of Mr. Schreiner. The Court did not allow defense adequate time to investigate the accusation, nor did defense counsel investigate, even later, to make a connection between the victim and Mr. , nor between Mr. and his accuser Mr. . In reading the file documents of what little was investigated, I can make a connection between and through convicted murderer . Police reported that 's relative visited inmate , who was then incarcerated for homicide, during Ms. Schreiner's trial, and asked why had accused of killing Mr. Schreiner. told he would take care of it. This conversation was recorded and lasted 77 minutes. No reasonable doubt theories were presented by trial counsel, nor was any further investigation conducted.

Mr. Draggon – as a defense alternate suspect

Mr. Draggon was the Schreiners' residence at the time of the homicide. Ms. Schreiner tried to convince her trial attorneys before trial that Mr. Draggon may have killed her husband, yet defense counsel did not investigate her accusation, nor present him in any way to raise reasonable doubt.

I interviewed Mr. Draggon in 2008. Mr. Draggon is a self-proclaimed "mentally disabled" person. (I found him to be emotionally unstable during my second interview with him, during which he cried, cursed at me, demonized Ms. Schreiner over and over again all in the same sentence.) His first interview with me was very calm and controlled. Mr. Draggon wore what looked to me like pink toenail polish. Mr. Draggon informed me that he has PTSD from some childhood event in which is why he "had to escape" from there, so he moved to Vermont , and that he had "been in therapy for years."

He admitted to me that he was on June 2, 2004 (the day of the homicide). He admitted to me that he used Zolpidem (Ambien) at that time. He admitted to me that he hated Ms. Schreiner, and often fought with her verbally. He stated Mr. Schreiner often apologized for his wife. My interview of the Schreiners' close friend Richard X. indicated, however, that Richard X. witnessed Mr. Draggon and Mr. Schreiner (not Mrs. Schreiner) having verbal confrontations. Mr. X. characterized Mr. Draggon as unstable and angry, and Mr. Schreiner as having a sharp tongue. Mr. X. witnessed Mr. Draggon yell at both of the Schrieners using very "foul language." Mr. X. was upset that Ms. Schreiner's attorneys never asked him about Mr. Draggon at trial.

Vermont medical examiner Steven Shafer, M.D. also indicated that the decedent looked to have been in a fist fight. It is very possible that Mr. Draggon and Mr. Schreiner again became confrontational (Mr. Schreiner also having had ingested Ambien would be wobbly and physically unstable), and that Mr. Draggon lost control and struck Mr. Schreiner. Ms. Schreiner had no fresh wounds on her hands, face, or arms.

Trial counsel, ignoring the request of their client to investigate Mr. Draggon, never investigated Mr. Draggon nor presented him to raise reasonable doubt at trial.

LACK OF INVESTIGATION – Failure to interview witnesses

While trial counsel did depose some of the State's experts, they only interviewed two witnesses for defense, Richard and Donna X.

Richard & Donna X.

Trial counsel did depose Mr. and Mrs. X., but only with regard to time of death. They were on the Schreiner property for a few minutes between 10:30am and 11:30am on the day of the homicide, and did not notice the deceased. Counsel could have, but did not, utilize Mr. X. as a character witness for Mrs. Schreiner. Prosecution intimated at trial that Mrs. Schreiner perhaps wanted to kill her husband and run off with her lover Paul Driftwood, however, Mr. X. told me that Mr. Schreiner already knew about the affair and did not care about it. Mr. Schreiner also told Mr. X. that Ms. Schreiner was free to leave him if and whenever she wanted to with no hard feelings on his part, and that they had it all worked out to build a new house and live on separate floors in that house. Mrs. Schreiner never gave Mr. X. the impression that she wanted to leave her marriage. Mr. X. also stated that Mr. and Mrs. Schreiner got along just fine. Mr. X. was upset that Mrs. Schreiner's attorneys never asked him about Mr. Draggon at trial, nor did they offer him as a character witness for their client. Mr. X. believes Mrs. Schreiner is innocent, and he believes her attorneys didn't do much in defense of her. He called the trial "a farce."

Gaylyn Schreiner

Again ignoring their client's request, defense counsel never interviewed Mrs. Schreiner's daughter-in-law Gaylyn Schreiner who spoke with the State's key lay witnesses [redacted] Rowe. Rowe stated that Mrs. Schreiner confessed "I did it" to her while in a room full of policeman on the day of the crime and told police of this confession in the days following, having awoke in the middle of the night and recalled the confession. Gaylyn Schreiner later had a conversation with Ms. Rowe in which Rowe confessed she felt intimidated and perhaps even coerced by police when she told police of that statement by Mrs. Schreiner. She felt the police pressured her into offering some evidence against Mrs. Schreiner. Ms. Rowe told Gaylyn she was afraid of the police and did not want to talk with them again. Gaylyn, whose husband is an attorney [redacted], [redacted] also stated that when she called Mrs. Schreiner on the day of the homicide just after hearing of Mr. Schreiner's death, police answered the phone and would not allow her to speak with Mrs. Schreiner.

LACK OF INVESTIGATION – Failure to adequately communicate with client

During my conversations with Mrs. Schreiner, she told me that her trial counsel did not discuss defense strategy with her in any way. Mrs. Schreiner also complained to me that trial counsel did not honor her requests to interview her therapist (to learn that she was not angry nor wanting to leave or hurt her husband), Gaylyn Schreiner (to mitigate [redacted] Rowe's statements against Mrs. Schreiner), or Mr. Draggon (who Mrs. Schreiner believes killed Mr. Schreiner). Mrs. Schreiner did not fully understand what was happening at trial, nor why she was not asked to take the stand in her own defense. It is Mrs. Schreiner's contention that trial counsel were not experienced and were distracted with personal issues, such as divorce, a [redacted] husband, and other personal matters.

CONCLUSION

If I had been the pre-trial defense investigator for Mrs. Schreiner, prosecution's time of death theory would have been quickly refuted by defense expert witnesses and time of death would have been established during a time in which Mrs. Schreiner had a solid alibi. Additionally, prosecution's theory of motive would have been dispelled at trial through the additional testimony of Richard X. Reasonable doubt would have been presented by illuminating Paul [redacted], [redacted], and, most importantly, Mr. Draggon as viable alternate suspects. In doing so, Ms. Schreiner would likely have been acquitted at trial. Post-conviction news reports indicated that jurors did not feel there was enough evidence to convict on first degree homicide, so they convicted on second degree homicide. I contend that they convicted at all merely because trial counsel did not perform adequately.

I swear under penalty of perjury that the foregoing is true to the best of my information and belief.

Signed this ___ day of August, 2009.

After writing the affidavit and offering it to Mrs. Schreiner's post-conviction counsel, I never learned whether he presented it or any of the information it contained to the court on Mrs. Schreiner's behalf. This post-conviction counsel preferred not to communicate much with me or keep me apprised of the status of the case. What I do know is this: Hope remained in jail and never was awarded a new trial.

Hope's trial attorneys got one thing right for sure; they condemned law enforcement for trampling through the crime scene, not using gloves, failing to search comprehensively, and for targeting Ms. Schreiner and no other person as their suspect from day one.

Hope made the fatal error of granting law enforcement an interview. Police found bloody towels in the trash, and she continued to clean up blood literally while speaking with police, which act was later used against her in court as trying to get rid of evidence. Really? While standing next to police and talking to them, she washed her sneakers and bloody towel which she had wiped her hands on after administering CPR.

In her interviews with police, she said Bob was controlling and emotionally abusive. Her statements were later used against her in court as additional motive, along with the affair. I'm not an attorney, so I do not give legal advice. However, I do state my agreement with the best attorneys who tell their clients not to speak with law enforcement, especially without first consulting an attorney. You do not have to!

In my case experience, speaking to police, even when the client merely professes innocence and nothing else, has always come back to hurt them at trial. Those innocent statements are always twisted and used against defendants without exception, in my experience.

A relationship counselor once told me "never complain and never explain." It only creates more drama and is often misunderstood.

The local newspaper reported that the judge presiding over Hope's trial told the court audience during sentencing that those who believed Hope Schreiner was innocent were "in denial," citing blood and DNA evidence trailing from the body into the house.

I say that one would expect this trail of blood to occur simply from Hope finding the body, going into the house to call 911, and then back outside and attempting CPR on her husband . . . not to mention the cat and multiple police officers that were improperly walking through the bloody scene into the house.

The judge further said that Hope killed her husband in a "savage and brutal" attack that shocked the very small community. To me, those words profiled Draggon, not 73-year-old Ms. Schreiner, who had a solid alibi for the most logical time of death.

Two years ago (nine years after my work on the case), yet another new attorney for Hope contacted me and asked what my investigation uncovered. This phone call alerted me to the potential that the previous post-conviction counsel never presented my affidavit to the court.

New counsel accepted my affidavit via email and thanked me for my insights. The court granted Hope Schreiner permanent medical leave, in effect parole, shortly thereafter.

As the second eldest incarcerated person in the State of Vermont, Hope experienced multiple ailments and a broken hip during her incarceration. She is now living in Vermont in a supervised adult-living facility, walking in the sunshine, and gardening. She has had no unusual ailments since her release from prison.

By writing letters in support of Hope's release, my mother and at least one of Hope's children helped champion her release. To this day, I have no idea whether or not my affidavit was ever presented to a court or the parole board.

Formerly well off financially, Hope now has no money because of legal fees, and the kids fighting over her share of the family estate. When convicted of her husband's death, Hope's lifelong interests were forfeited by law at the time her appeals were exhausted.

Sadly, the Schreiner family is vastly divided. My mother is likely Hope's closest and most consistent contact.

Hope has formally authorized me to write about her case. Although she has reviewed these chapters and approved them for accuracy, she stated it would be too painful to add comment about her personal experiences with her family throughout the ordeal, and so she declined to do so.

The Innocence Project of Florida reports that women facing criminal charges in the United States often face gender-based bias resulting in the "vilification of a woman on the grounds that the crime was committed out of passion, rage, or another archaic nonsensical reason that parrots stereotypes of characteristics of women." [10]

According to the Bluhm Legal Clinic's Center on Wrongful Convictions at Northwestern Law School, "In 64 percent of female exonerees' cases, no crime had occurred," and "40 percent of female exonerees were victims of police or prosecutorial misconduct."

My friend recently had a problem with oil leaking from her car. She took the vehicle to a local repair business and was informed the motor needed to be removed in order to replace the oil pan. Then she went for a second opinion from someone recommended. He laughed and fixed the problem in less than an hour. It's a very good thing, for me, that my father taught me how to tune up my old Nissan 280-Z. To this day, when I need something fixed on my vehicle and don't know how to do it myself, I look up a YouTube video on the subject. It's not rocket science, ladies.

However, the unfortunate fact remains that some people don't believe women belong in a "man's world." Women are too often stereotyped as over-emotional and inept. I see things are changing, for the better. As I write this book, we have a female nominee for the presidency of the United States, and women in other government and corporate leadership positions. Hopefully, upcoming generations will continue to annihilate the antiquated negative stereotypes of women and of all bias against persons based on gender, sexuality, and race.

CASES IN THE NEWS
Cynthia Sommer

In 2002, Cynthia Sommer was charged with murder after allegedly poisoning her husband with arsenic. Although a medical examiner concluded Todd Sommer actually died of a heart attack, Cynthia Sommer was tried, convicted, and imprisoned. On appeal, Sommer's new defense attorney filed a motion for a new trial that was granted on the basis that trial counsel had deprived Sommer of a fair trial by opening the door for the prosecution to present inflammatory evidence of Sommer's behavior following her husband's death. New counsel also obtained additional tissue samples of the deceased which prosecution had not turned over to defense pre-trial. The samples were tested and proved that Todd Sommer was not poisoned at all. Her case was dismissed in 2013.

All legal claims by Sommer to collect reimbursement for legal expenses and punitive damages for wrongful incarceration were denied. [11]

Advertising Dollars: Media

In my free time, I used to watch tons of sports on TV, mostly National Football League games. I was a fantasy football commissioner for three years. The church of the NFL, I called it, every Sunday . . . and Monday . . . and Thursday sometimes.

As a kid, I watched lots of boxing and almost every sporting contest I found on television. Although I prefer documentaries, I started watching TV news, commentary, and legal shows in 2005. I had never been politically active or even interested. Anne was very politically charged, so I followed the 2008 presidential campaigns very closely with her, finding myself drawn to the candidates and the drama of their campaigns.

After the 2008 presidential election ended, that was the end of TV silliness for me. I simply decided my brain was so garbled with trash and contradictions from multiple news sources (liberal CNN, conservative FOX, and all the other news programs leeching off the major ones). No one was telling the whole truth, only giving his or her one-sided perspective. No one could be trusted. It was all garbage to me. There were also many negative, scary stories that I didn't need bringing me down constantly. I stopped watching TV completely in 2009.

It's been over seven years now. I don't read newspapers very often, and, only now and then do I follow up on a headline that I catch over the Internet. I'd never exposed myself to so much television news before, and most likely never will again.

I have to say, my mind is so much clearer, and I feel so much more peaceful since turning off the television. I do miss sports, but I have a lot more free time without the TV. I got my life back. I don't let my kids watch regular TV either. I'm sure they get enough of it at their dad's on the weekends, and I prefer that their young minds not be continuously bombarded with outsiders' opinions and criticisms of who they should be, and what their world is about. I try to limit their social media, but that seems impossible these days when every kid in school has a tablet and an iPhone.

I enjoy watching forensic and legal-based documentaries, but criminal law and live media simply don't mix well, in my opinion. Media outlets survive by portraying everything dramatically—and typically it's infused with a lot of bias.

When it comes to criminal law, the media, through television news or newspaper articles, is the outsiders' eyes into the case. Readers learn about a case from what's published in the news, on TV, and in books, much of which is incorrect and/or incomplete, unless it comes directly from an original source.

Publishing and/or televising anything about a defendant by name or photo, criminal charges, or ongoing legal battles in court, although interesting to viewers, can inadvertently taint the outcomes of criminal trials. Folks do not seem to appreciate the fact that what they see, hear, and read in the media is not the whole case, is sometimes biased, and is often inaccurate. And for the poor person newly arrested, that stigma—even if they win at trial or get their case dismissed—often tarnishes them unfairly. The arrest report stays on the innocent person's file.

As the defense investigator, I know the case facts. The defense attorneys know the case facts. The prosecutor knows most of case facts. The jurors and judge only know some of the case facts. There are actual facts and there are "trial facts." Trial facts are the bits of information allowed into a trial, and they are rarely if ever all of the actual facts of a case.

The attorneys and prosecutors present as many of the case facts supporting their arguments as are allowed in accordance with the rules of court—as many as the judge allows them to present. Many facts learned through my investigation are not presented in court, due to either legal strategy or legal restrictions for presenting certain evidence (or bad lawyering).

Rape shield laws are good examples. The defense team cannot present evidence that might generate prejudice against the victim based on his or her past behavior. I agree with this. Simply because a victim was promiscuous, or even went on a date with the accused, leading him all the way up to the point of entry, if you will, does not mean that "no" should be ignored. It is rape.

"No" means no. This is law in The United States. Even a husband must put on the brakes, as he can be charged with rape if he forces himself on his wife.

Another example of relevant evidence that we sometimes cannot present because it is prejudicial to the victim is prior violent history. If the defendant did not personally know the victim's history, then it cannot be presented in court as a fear present in the defendant's mind at the time of the incident. This was a major issue in the motorcycle-gang shooting case I mentioned earlier.

Our client, Mr. Y., shot a biker—one who happened to be driving a car at the time, not a motorcycle. He didn't know the victim, so could not have known the victim was historically violent.

I investigated the victim's history (court records, police reports, cell text messages, social media) and discovered that the victim was the president of a biker club chapter—the regional territory president of a national club. He had prior gun possession charges and domestic violence charges. His photos on social media showed him throwing gang signs and holding weapons. None of this evidence is allowed in at trial.

The brilliant defense attorney managed to present it all, however, by inference. Without breaking any rules of evidence, she got it in through the victim's friends at the scene, who stated that they were members of a biker club; through cops who were trained to address bikers as weapon-carrying persons; and through the victim's friends who admitted that they, and the victim himself, were not legally permitted to carry firearms. Why? Because felons cannot legally carry guns!

The defense attorney had the victim's friends and other witnesses describe the biker's "club" emblems on the victim's black leather vest, and explain that they were pledging for him that night during the club initiation process.

Do you think he had a violent history? Do you think his appearance and the public's general knowledge of bikers, especially ones who are in a parking lot threatening you, are reasonably perceived as dangerous? The defendant did, and so did the jury.

After the reading of the not guilty verdict, the jury sent a message to the judge telling him that they wanted to be escorted out of the courthouse in fear of the victim's friends and family. Had defense counsel not invented a legal way to get in all the history that was uncovered on these guys, the jurors would never have known how threatening the victim really was, and jurors might not have agreed with us that his friends left his body for a few minutes for some suspicious reason, like tossing a weapon before EMS arrived.

Let me give you some examples of media reporting errors. (I will be paraphrasing.) Let me also first say that many reporters misreport either because they simply do not understand what is important in a criminal matter, or they reprint unreliable statements—much like writing a story based only on police reports.

One of my favorites: "The victim was shot from behind multiple times." The readers went ballistic on social media posts speaking out against our client, Mr. Z.

"He shot the guy in the back!" "This is not self-defense!" "Murderer!" In this case, the media read the word "posterior" in the autopsy report and ignorantly ran with it as shot in the back. Or did they intentionally create a big stir in the community with the goal of selling newspapers?

There was no due diligence on the part of the reporter or editor to understand the anatomical definition of "posterior," which means to the rear of midline. Let us say that for our simple illustrative purposes here that midline runs downward from the ear, delineating front side and backside (anterior and posterior). A victim could be facing the shooter and ever-so-slightly turned to one side and be shot posterior of midline, meaning at an angle just behind the ear even though the victim is facing the shooter. This gets reported as "shot in the back" or "shot from behind."

In Mr. Z.'s case this negligent reporting went viral in the local community, causing our client to be considered guilty of murder by the media long before his court trial ever began.

The daily reporting of the trial was equally uninformed and misreported.

Consider this example: "The witness observed the defendant's car leave the scene." This is presumptuous, when in fact the witness saw "a" car that the police later believed to be the defendant's car. It was never proved to be the defendant's car. Ever. In fact, another suspect had the same type of car as the defendant. Both drove dark wood-paneled station wagons with loud mufflers.

"There was blood on the headlights of the defendant's car." Yes, there was. Animal blood. He hit a goose. The feathers were still in the headlight sockets.

Too often media people report without adequate information or understanding, and inadvertently (or perhaps intentionally) publicly crucify a defendant before a jury hears the case. This is one reason I don't watch TV news. Too much of it is biased, misreported, not researched, or simply mistaken. Then we all get wound up over something that is not even true. A good journalist will vet (investigate) the "facts" they are given before reporting them.

News media companies are in the business of selling newspapers or television time, and higher ratings draw in higher advertising dollars. We watch media that is exciting and evokes emotion in us, *à la* Nancy Grace.

Often these commentator shows come only from one perspective, which is fine, but they sometimes involve erroneous or biased reporting in the process. They're in the business of sensationalism, and there are few repercussions for an erroneous and damaging media report.

How does a defendant then get a fair jury after a big news media and social media explosion? Why should media be allowed to use a citizen's actual name and photo before they are convicted? When it turns out they're innocent, the damage to their reputation is already done, without apology.

One of my clients facing child sexual-assault charges, whose name was in newspaper articles, television, and online news sites, lost his job three different times before the trial even took place. Once a new employer caught wind of his pending criminal case, he was released from the job.

He finally had to move two hours from his home and family in order to continue to work to support them. He was a highly educated and skilled engineer. I believed him to be completely innocent. After over two years of hell for him, all charges were dismissed.

Please remember that media, confessions, and polygraphs, especially those done by law enforcement on a suspect or witness, are not always reliable sources of information.

As a criminal defense investigator I am an original source of information. Yes, a witness can lie to me, so I cannot vouch for a witness's truthfulness. I am, however, the original source of my investigation experiences and discoveries. When I talk about my own experiences you're getting firsthand information and my recollection of how witnesses personally interacted with me.

Do you really think that you know all the evidence that existed in the O.J. Simpson trial? Not even the jury heard all the evidence. Could you agree in any way that the media reporting of that trial was even a little sensationalized, focused on increasing viewership? What sells us on media? Drama.

It seems like common sense to me that getting the facts should be about getting all the facts. While I'm being harsh, please understand that my criticisms are intended to target only erroneous, unethical, sensationalized, and negligent media reporting. Certainly, there are honest and informed reporters and broadcasters . . . or at least those who intend to be diligent in reporting the news.

It is important, in my opinion, to view all secondary information with great caution.

Good Cop, Bad Cop

No system can be just if humans make the decisions. This is the sad reality presented in this book. The focus of my work and the purpose of this book is to help bring balance to an off-kilter criminal justice system.

I'm not in the business of setting criminals free. My purpose is to help protect all citizens from the human error and greed that exist within the justice system.

How many people have been falsely accused? Millions, I'm sure. The National Registry of Exonerations indicates that 149 people were exonerated in the United States last year alone (2015). [12]

Those were rare cases that made it out of the system after conviction.

It is further reported through the Registry that those exonerated served an average of 14.5 years of incarceration. These people were innocent! How does this happen? Why are wrongful convictions so prevalent? Where does the system go wrong?

Cops can usually see through false allegations quite readily, though not always. Sometimes their emotions get in the way.

Sometimes selfish agendas get in the way.

This happened on the child sexual assault case I mentioned above, in which my client lost his job three times. To me, just reading the 11-year-old's initial one-paragraph handwritten statement and watching the video of her initial police interview, it was clear that the adolescent was lying.

The police didn't see it, or maybe there was pressure to prosecute the case. The girl's mother was very angry. The mother was also my client's ex-girlfriend. He had broken up with her. This fact alone does not, by any means, imply that the allegation was false. But in this case, it was.

The child's therapist should never have talked to me, but she did. After interviewing the therapist for three hours and researching the girl's school records and medical records (which we subpoenaed), it was clear that the girl was a pathological liar who had mental health issues due to traumatic brain injury as a toddler.

I surmised that even though the girl's mother knew she was a liar, she wanted to believe the girl's allegations against the boyfriend who dumped her.

The original prosecutor would not dismiss the case even though we presented evidence that the 11-year-old was lying. The prosecutor was new to the position, and apparently, he was trying to prove that he was tough on crime.

Defense counsel filed a motion to postpone the trial (based on another issue), and the motion was granted. The attorney wisely delayed the trial until after the end of the year's elections, hoping the current prosecutor would not be re-elected. Thankfully, he wasn't re-elected. The new prosecutor agreed that the girl was lying and withdrew the charges. Yay for good prosecutors!

People convicted in child sexual-assault cases often receive harsher sentences than those convicted of murder. A sentence of life in prison is not uncommon at all. There are often no witnesses and no physical evidence of assault, but only a "he-said she-said." Sexual assault cases, especially involving minors, are emotionally charged, for obvious reasons.

How many people have been wrongly convicted? I don't know the number. No one does.

The Innocence Project at Cardozo Law School in New York City cites well over 300 exonerations due to later DNA testing alone, including just over 150 death row inmates.

"According to the Innocence Project's estimates, between 2.3 percent and 5 percent of all U.S. prisoners are innocent." The United States inmate population fluctuates around two million. Using these numbers, as many as 100,000 innocent people could currently be wrongly incarcerated. [13]

Think of all the innocent people sitting in jail that don't have the luxury of a good defense team. How can all of this happen with such dreadful frequency?

My answer: the frailty of human nature. I'm not talking about people accused of crimes. Instead, I'm talking about the people investigating, advocating, and prosecuting cases against citizens.

Humans are the weak links in the otherwise strong armor of justice; they are the cancer in an otherwise healthy host. The ugliness of human nature—greed, lethargy, apathy, and bias—all seriously compromise the potential for a true and just legal system. Wouldn't it be wonderful if we would all do the right thing and support the truth regardless of how it affects our personal agendas?

The National Registry for Exonerations reported that in 2015, 65 exonerations were known to include official misconduct. Further, three-quarters of exonerations included official misconduct in wrongfully convicting persons accused of homicide.

Even if we put all the evidence into a computer to decide a defendant's fate, a human programmed the computer and uploaded the evidence. There's no way to avoid failure in a system of people judging people.

Of course, in a perfect world, there would be no need for defense. The only truth, the "God" in this system, lives in each of our hearts. The system "as is" is set up to allow corruption even though that certainly is not what was intended.

Take a moment to consider the persecution of Max Roybal. Over a four-year period, seven government agencies on the side of the prosecution investigated the Laura Cecere homicide: the Oak Grove Police Department, Criminal Investigations Unit at Fort Campbell, Tennessee Bureau of Investigations, the FBI, Clarksville Police Department, Sumner County Sheriff's Department, and the Tennessee Highway Patrol.

One defense investigator blew holes in their entire case so wide that a judge actually intervened mid-trial and dismissed all charges.

How can this happen? This was my first homicide investigation. I wasn't experienced. They were.

Why didn't all these highly trained law enforcement officers and prosecution team members vet their evidence in the same way I vetted it? How could all these officials have been so driven to get their man that they didn't bother to make certain it was the right man? And if Max was the right man, shouldn't they have found some real evidence to prove it? Did they simply assume the jury would convict based only on emotion and sympathy for the victim?

I have great sympathy for the victim and her family, and yet I feel no shame in holding the prosecution to its burden of proof. How did the state protect citizens in Roybal's cases? The state investigated over a span of four years, and still law enforcement officers found no reliable evidence leading to who killed Laura Cecere. Did they investigate anyone other than Mr. Roybal? No. Karen Anderson was likely not murdered at all, but they dug her body up anyway.

I have worked cases in which prosecutors gave jailhouse snitches lighter sentences in exchange for testimony against the defendant. I worked on a case in which a prosecutor entered into a plea deal with a co-defendant who admittedly participated in the brutal sexual assault and homicide of a 14-year-old girl. After the rape, the perpetrators tied the girl to a tree and left her in the woods. Hikers later found her bones. Her bones bore the marks of animal teeth.

The prosecutor let the co-defendant go FREE in exchange for her testimony against the other defendant. Thankfully, I did not have the task of investigating innocence in this case.

It's no wonder I have nightmares. Cases like this make my job difficult on a personal level, and I have to focus much harder on the greater good I'm doing in preserving all citizens' rights.

Defense attorneys can be blamed for many failures in the legal system as well.

The young man mentioned earlier, Mr. Y., shot and killed an aggressive biker club member in self-defense. Without completing an investigation, his original defense attorney pled him out to second-degree murder merely because the client was black and was facing trial in a white rural city. The attorney never gave the investigator the case discovery to review. Very minimal investigation could be done.

With a new attorney in place, Mr. Y. won his request for a new trial based on ineffective assistance of counsel. The case proceeded to trial, and after comprehensive defense investigation and with a talented attorney, he was acquitted of all charges.

This clearly illustrates the value of a thorough investigation, coupled with intelligent and zealous advocacy, in comparison to the prior result where defense counsel did not adequately represent the same client.

Many cases go to trial without adequate, or even any, defense investigation. That should be a crime in and of itself. I have investigated multiple post-conviction homicide cases in which minimal or no investigation was ever done on the defendant's behalf before trial. Needless to say, the defendants were convicted, guilty or not.

Attorneys cannot testify, and who is going to believe a client accused of murder? Some jurors tend to believe a defendant is guilty simply because the defendant was arrested.

Through my professional experience, I have been made aware of despicable acts of corruption and gross negligence on both sides of the justice system. I have known defense counsel who exchanged legal services for blow jobs. One such attorney, in fact, had the audacity to tell me of his arrangement with a woman in a child custody battle. According to him, she reneged on the oral copulation, and thus he didn't file her papers to maintain custody of her children.

While he was bragging to me about his sweet revenge, we were in the midst of a capital post-conviction defense of a man who should never have received the death penalty.

Counsel openly hated our client. I loved the client. He is one of my all-time favorites. He killed his wife. He never denied it. He was heartbroken over it. It wasn't premeditated. Although I did find some exculpatory evidence for the post-conviction hearing, this attorney decided not to present it. We lost. The client is still on death row awaiting a wrongful execution.

I also know a private investigator who I perceive as being more interested in socializing with his female staff than gaining important interviews in support of his clients. He hired me as a new investigator while I was working on the Shakir case. When he found out I was gay, he instantly "let me go." This was how I ended up going out on my own, and how I got my very first case. The client replaced him with me. Ha!

Yes, I sued his ass. However, I chickened out on the gay thing, never mentioning it in my wrongful termination claim. We settled. I regret not bringing out the truth as I saw it, but I was not ready to make a statement like that at the time. I have never felt that being gay (or bi) is something that needed to stand out about me. I'm a loving person. That is my preferred label.

My metaphysical gurus proclaim adversity is always a

blessing in disguise. Indeed it was.

Case in point: my former investigator boss, we will call him Investigator Suave, arranged to interview the mother of two young girls who accused the client of touching them inappropriately. The charges carried a 37-year sentence for the defendant. Thirty-seven years for touching?

Suave visited the home of the mother of the alleged victims, and knocked on the door. She refused to grant him an interview. That was the end of it. He tried no more.

I was then hired by the defendant. I knocked on the mother's door. When she first opened the door to me, just a crack, I explained why I was there and she refused to speak with me. I quickly turned her attention to her garden and complimented her on its beauty, asking how she got it all to bloom so well when mine is a disaster. She opened the crack in the door a bit wider. It was clear she welcomed compliments, so I asked her for more gardening advice. After a little more coaxing, she opened the door completely and we moved from a conversation about her garden to her children and the allegations against my new client.

She divulged important information withheld by the prosecutor about undisclosed interviews with the children, as well as about sexual abuse and anger in her own childhood. At the time of the allegations, the mother and the defendant were hanging out in a hot tub together. It turned out that the defendant did not want to date her. She wanted an apology. What mother would only ask for an apology if she truly believed her children had been molested?

Law enforcement has a long public history of corruption.

During my work on the Jamal Shakir case in South Central Los Angeles, the local communities there were still reeling from the recent Rampart scandal.

"The LAPD Rampart scandal refers to widespread corruption in the Community Resources Against Street Hoodlums (CRASH) anti-gang unit of the Los Angeles Police Department's Rampart Division in the late 1990s. More than 70 police officers who were either assigned to or associated with the Rampart CRASH unit were implicated in some form of misconduct, making it one of the most widespread cases of documented police misconduct in United States history, responsible for a long list of offenses including unprovoked shootings, unprovoked beatings, planting of false evidence, frame-ups, stealing and dealing narcotics, bank robbery, perjury, and the covering up of evidence of these activities." [14]

This was happening in an already downtrodden community of impoverish black and Hispanic families. The people we trust to serve and protect us were taking advantage of the weak and helpless. Despicable.

I attended a community meeting in Los Angeles at which the police department spokesperson fielded angry verbal assaults and "what are we gonna do about this" questions from local townspeople. It was a very heated conversation, as you might imagine . . . and historically not at all unfamiliar to citizens and law enforcement in the U.S.

Police officers stand on the front lines of community carnage and recover millions of dollars' worth of dope. Gangsters get rich while the officers risk their lives for an average salary. It has to be incredibly disheartening to keep putting the same person through the system time and time again, cleaning up the bodies along the way. It's endless. Senseless.

Even so, the people we employ to serve and protect us, must remain steadfast in the pursuit of true justice; protecting and serving diligently, honestly, and without personal agendas and bias.

One of my cases arose when two gang unit cops chased a Hispanic man into a mobile home and tasered him for no legal reason. Do you realize that people can die from being tasered?

The cops merely assumed the guy was up to no good because he "fit the gangbanger profile." When the two cops then learned the Hispanic man was unarmed, the bad cop searched the guy's house, found a gun in his bedroom, and placed it underneath the innocent citizen lying motionless on the entry hall floor.

The bad cop then wrote a report stating that he believed the armed Hispanic suspect broke into a home to burglarize it, and so he chased and subdued him. What the officers did not know, however, was that the guy was married with kids and was entering his own home after getting a ride from a friend.

How do I know the bad cop planted the evidence and falsified the report? His partner ratted him out in court! The "good" cop could not live with what his partner had done. It was clear they had no reason to chase my client into his own home and assault him. They profiled an innocent man and illegally assaulted him, in his own home nonetheless. They reported that the man broke into the home by pushing in the front door. Yet the front door opened to the outside. That was a very careless lie for the bad officer to report.

Now this citizen can sue the county, and likely will win money damages. This is a case of taxpayers' money going to waste because cops sometimes behave like gangsters.

The officers chosen to protect us should be vetted for strength of character, a proven track record of good mental health, financial stability, a proven history of personal integrity, and good physical health—especially a good heart.

Several years ago, defense counsel on a death penalty case hired me to research the myriad violent gangs that sprouted up in the United States. My task was to learn about gang culture and search for mitigation witnesses in support of our client during sentencing. The purpose was to appeal to the judge for relief from capital punishment based on the hardships the client had endured.

I found myself once again entering maximum-security state prisons and interviewing leaders of violent local street gangs and international mafia. In addition, I spent the better part of eight months out in the streets interviewing witnesses to shootings as well as active and inactive gang members who were not incarcerated. Researching gang life on this level was interesting to me.

My "star" witness, an imprisoned, formerly violent street gang leader, was now a humble man who agreed to help us. A few days after my second visit with my wonderful witness, I took a call from the attorney while I was in the middle of a music recording session. She told me my witness had just been murdered in prison.

By asking so many questions, I was certain I'd stirred up some old stuff for these folks, but this news hit me hard.

Just a few days prior to the prison murder, I reached one mysterious leader, who only spoke with me on the phone after I located and talked with his parents, who passed my number on to him.

I wondered whether this other man, who wasn't incarcerated but was the gang co-leader with my witness back when, was concerned that my witness would say too much. This other man had a frightening reputation and was still on the streets somewhere.

I had never experienced anything like this before, something so close to me out in the field. I looked over my shoulder the entire night and next day. I searched the closets and under the bed of my hotel room and double-locked the door.

My brother, who is the executor of my estate, heard my long-lost voice on the other end of the phone as I informed him of what happened, and that I would be sending him updated documents on all my personal and financial dealings.

Figuring I needed to find another witness for the case, I spent the next day re-interviewing another man for the task. Honestly, I felt partly responsible for my guy's murder, and I think I was in a state of shock at that point, just going through the motions like a zombie on autopilot.

The other investigators on the case informed me that prisoners work the prison. They handle the paperwork. They knew I was there. I had no idea. I was concerned for my other witnesses and for myself, and so I informed the team I was going home for a weekend to recover.

The attorneys emailed back that we were continuing with the investigation and instructed us to all keep working. I again replied that I was not comfortable putting any witnesses in jeopardy and was taking a couple days off.

I then received a phone call from the attorney who asked me, quite pointedly, "What part of 'we are continuing the investigation' don't you understand?"

Her tone was reminiscent of my father in my youth, and it triggered a knee-jerk response in me. I realize I'm just a lowly defense investigator, but I do not like being disrespected.

I responded, "What part of 'no' don't YOU understand? I'll be back on Monday," and I ended the call without acquiescing to her demands. I guess I was a little wound up.

I don't think this attorney has spoken to me since that phone call, and we're talking many years ago. Ahh, the anxiety of attorneys before a big trial. Her passion was obvious, and a necessary quality in representing the client well.

We discovered that someone, the prosecutor or corrections people or law enforcement, was messing with us. Our guy was still alive and well.

The attorney of whom I speak is a very compassionate and intelligent attorney. Her closing speech during the sentencing phase of the trial was breathtaking. She put two of my witnesses on the stand to help her argue against a death sentence for the client. She cares about her clients, she is experienced, and she was very eloquent in court.

We achieved our goal: a sentence of life without parole in lieu of the death penalty. Her inappropriate outburst on the phone with me that day illustrated the familiar intensity of attorneys heading into an important trial. The task is daunting and stressful, especially in capital cases.

That said, far too many attorneys don't value or appreciate their investigators enough. The very best attorneys, in my opinion, know the value of a good defense investigator and partner with them in brainstorming on legal strategy throughout a case. This is the most effective way to collaborate, and the best way to get the most out of an investigator.

The investigator must know all the issues related to the charges and which evidence is important to support defense strategies. Investigators also need to understand the nuances of the law, which the attorney can best impart. Then the investigators can do their work and provide a more competent investigation.

Without this level of collaboration, defense investigators are merely used as errand runners and the case might not be as comprehensively examined as it could be. Not to mention, no experienced investigator appreciates being treated as a mere underling.

Unfortunately, I have seen a shocking level of official misconduct and carelessness in the cases I have reviewed. I've worked cases involving law enforcement prejudice and bias, as well as the planting of evidence. I've seen cases pushed through with incomplete investigation due to community and media pressures, and numerous instances of inexperience or incompetence—including failure to collect important physical incident scene evidence, failure to properly secure an incident scene, and failure to conduct a thorough investigation.

There are plenty of proven instances of forensic lab errors and misconduct as well. All of this, in addition to simple honest errors. Mistakes, inexperience, and incompetence are not necessarily malicious, but simply human error.

Burnout, however, is inexcusable. Get off the job.

We all make mistakes, no matter how hard we're trying to be accurate and complete. The problem with making mistakes in this business is that people's lives hang in the balance. That's where the team effort is essential, and why it's important to have an attorney who is willing to collaborate with the investigator. The attorney and investigator keep each other in check.

Some people are intentionally malicious, even professionals in our legal system—on both sides. Both good and bad stewards of justice exist throughout the legal system.

I am being judgmental. There was a time that I chastised myself for doing so, but later I came to realize that I needed to be critical in my business. I shouldn't be demeaning, but I should keep an eye out for things that appear out of place.

While I would welcome the opportunity to work with a good prosecutor, I don't ever want to be a cop on the streets. Not because I don't trust myself to maintain my integrity, but because I'm not willing to risk my life on the front lines and I certainly don't want to ever have to shoot anybody. My mother calls me a pacifist. I guess that's accurate. Experienced and honest police men and women who work to serve and empower all citizens are my heroes . . . thank you, thank you, thank you!

There are good men and women on both sides who do good work out in the streets, follow-up investigation, trial work, and then watch their cases fall through the cracks of a broken justice system. The criminal justice system works well on paper, but, again, it can't be a perfect system when people are relied upon to act with full integrity, put in great effort, and make unemotional life-altering decisions. This is why I do what I do. I don't fight for rapists and murderers. I fight for our system to work as intended.

I get a lot of flack because I work on the side of the defense. Or the "dark side," as law enforcement and prosecutors like to call it.

In my estimation, some of them are on the dark side. I'm out in rural wastelands, homeless camps, and drug-infested dark alleys at night. I don't have a badge to hide behind, and I don't have backup. I put myself at risk for the greater good too, though I admit I'm not on the front lines and in the sort of danger that law enforcement officers face every day at work. That said, a female criminal defense investigator was recently murdered in northern California.

Last year, I had lunch with a friend. I'm an avid poker player, and that's how we met. Don is now retired. He invites me to lunch at the casino buffet where he is a high roller and gets lots of comps (free stuff). We catch up with one another during our periodic lunches and the occasional hike in the Sierra Mountains. So while eating together one day, he asked how things were going.

"Did you read the paper this week?" I asked.

"Yes."

"Did you read about the private investigator who found a missing bullet at the recent shooting homicide scene?"

"Yes, I did," he said. "Obviously they planted it there."

He meant that because a defense investigator, rather than a cop, found the bullet, the defense investigator must have planted the evidence in order to get the charges against the client dismissed (because cops don't miss evidence like that).

"I'm the private investigator in that case." [Pause] "Now, do you think that bullet was planted?" I challenged him.

"Huh? You are? No." He answered with his tail between his legs. "No, I don't."

Don knows I didn't plant that evidence. He's the perfect example of the way many people don't trust the defense. Everyone seems to be prosecutorial-minded.

Do we all live in fear of the bad person? Do we even know who he or she really is? Why don't we consider how common it is for people to be falsely accused? My guess is that we don't want to believe it. We need to feel safe. We need to feel like that could never happen to us. We don't want to believe that bad people sometimes wear badges, robes, and expensive suits.

Believe it.

Aside from winning cases for the good guys, the most satisfying rewards for my work are the texts and emails I receive from past clients. Yesterday I received one.

The client asked how I was, and thanked me again for the beautiful sunrise that he watched through the trees in his front yard again this morning. It makes me proud of what I have helped accomplish for some innocent folks.

This same client, who just texted me, hated the legal system because he had been wrongly accused. When he first met me, he thought I was just another uncaring, money-hungry, "defender pretender." He refused to shake my hand, and told me, "I don't like germs," only later to tell me how grateful he is, and that he will love me forever because I believed in him when no one else did. I fought for him even though we were strangers.

I'm proud to be a compassionate person, one who has helped preserve the freedom of innocent people who have been wrongfully accused of violent crimes. This is the heart of the matter. This is why I do what I do.

How safe would we all really be if there were no criminal defense attorneys and investigators?

Sedley Alley: Trial and Error

The Federal Public Defender in Nashville, Tennessee, hired me to investigate guilt/innocence on behalf of death row inmate Sedley Alley. At that point it was 18 years after a jury had convicted him of the exceptionally heinous rape and homicide of the daughter of a U.S. Ambassador.

Sedley Alley

Sedley sat on death row all this time without ever having the benefit of a defense investigator looking into his claims of innocence.

At the time of her death, the victim, Suzanne Collins, was a mere 19 years old. She was enrolled in aviation training school, and was a Lance Corporal in the Marines.

Similar to Mr. Roybal's case concerning the death of Laura Cecere, Sedley's ex-wife died prior to the homicide in question. Debra Alley was at home in the bathtub and choked on her vomit. No one was accused of murdering Ms. Alley until the horrible death of Suzanne Collins years later. Only then did officials come to the conclusion that Sedley was responsible for both deaths.

When I took on the Sedley Alley case, I was still a new investigator, only two years into my independent work. The Federal Defender in Nashville was Alley's last hope for justice. As the final federal habeas corpus hearing approached, the defense attorneys wanted to cross the investigation effort off the list of Alley's entitlements.

Habeas corpus is Latin for "you have the body." A habeas action in the legal world is a writ asking a judge to review a case, via a court hearing, to decide whether a person's freedom should be restricted. That is, the court must decide whether a person is imprisoned illegally. We informally call it "habeas."

There are both state and federal habeas hearings.

It was my impression that no one considered Alley innocent by any means. Not only did he confess to the killing, he spent time after his arrest in a mental hospital, having blamed the murder on hearing voices that told him to kill the teenage girl.

Mr. Alley's attorneys—competent and caring federal public defense attorneys—were working on mental health mitigation arguments that might commute Alley's death sentence to a life sentence without the opportunity for parole.

They led me into a room with four or more bankers' boxes related to the Alley case containing discovery documents and transcripts. The murder had occurred in 1985. I began my work on the case in 2003.

Sedley Alley's prior attorneys never conducted an

investigation into the allegations. Nothing.

I started reading, organizing documents, and making notes. One of the first items I saw was a photo of the pretty victim, Suzanne Collins. Although I didn't personally relate to Suzanne, I felt great empathy for her and her family.

A legal colleague of mine playfully calls me a "bleeding heart." My heart is not bleeding. It is full. I always feel empathy for victims. A homicide victim is a person whose life has ended. Whether the deceased was "good" or "bad" doesn't matter to me. Whether the death was the victim's own stupid fault, or whether the victim was an anti-social type, a gangster, an addict, or what have you doesn't matter to me.

I feel a similar empathy for defendants who might have killed the victim. It's a bad choice, obviously, to commit murder, unless in self-defense.

One client admitted he was a drug dealer and told me exactly what went down. The poor guy, still in his twenties, not strung out himself, faced well over a decade in prison. He decided to take a plea offer for less time in prison in exchange for becoming a confidential informant for police. This was a future life decision he already regretted, but the sobering alternative of a lengthy incarceration in state prison was even more intolerable. He regretted making such poor choices and ruining his life.

I know it's only because he was caught that he was remorseful, but still, you must feel something for these young people. He was an intelligent person with a family and, had he made better choices, a good life ahead of him.

Sitting behind bars with him and listening to him talk

candidly about all his mistakes—how he had trapped himself, ruined his life, failed his parents, and wished he could take it all back—I admit I felt a lot of compassion for him. When he made a strained and obvious attempt to hold back his building emotion, I felt compelled to console him. He appeared, to me, so scared and alone.

I never know if I'm going to get in trouble for hugging an inmate, but so far, I have not. He welcomed my gesture.

The moment he held onto me, his body started shaking and his tears poured out onto my shoulder. It broke my heart, but I was happy I could be there for this young man. He'd made a terrible mistake. I wish I could save every kid from going down such a dreadful path. I hope he turns his life around and inspires others to do better.

The Alley case was no different. Feel the emotions, let them pass, and then go to work.

Back to my banker's boxes. I sat and stared at the photo of the victim Suzanne Collins, who was allegedly raped and murdered by Sedley Alley in 1985. Suzanne was talented, smart, and beautiful. Her family must be completely devastated. What a waste. Such a loss. She had so much potential and life ahead of her at only 19 years old. Why does evil like this happen? The answer is likely a spiritual one.

While harming another person is deeply disturbing in every case, the psychology of the human mind, especially a psychotic one that instigates murder, to me, is fascinating. Hitler? Manson? Deeply disturbing, yet also compelling to consider the ways their brains misfired, and how their followers disassociated from their own "better angels" and aligned with these "evil" dogmas.

Then there is the temporary insanity of a crime of passion . . . very interesting and shocking. Rape and torture, not so interesting to me . . . merely pathetic. Being victimized, degraded, violated, robbed of one's choices and one's sacredness, then left to live with it, somehow seems worse than being murdered.

One of my earliest investigations was a rape kidnap case. My only task was to attempt an interview with the alleged victim. I persuaded her to speak with me in private, and I delineated the reasons she might not want to pursue the case to trial.

She later asked the prosecutor to offer a plea deal to the defendant, which he did.

How did I convince her? She told me that she saw handcuffs in the back seat of his car when she got into it. She went on a date with this stranger even after seeing the handcuffs. This fact would not go over well with a jury, and she would certainly be torn apart for it by the defense attorney at trial.

By the time I started my investigation, she really just wanted to forget about it. That interview was very hard for me to conduct so early on in my career. I felt deep sympathy for her, but I knew it would be worse for her at trial, and my job was to support the defense. I would have to find evidence to tear her apart.

Regarding Sedley Alley, I read that young Suzanne wanted to be a fighter pilot. I didn't know much about her childhood or short life, except that she was adopted, she was smart, all-American, virginal, accomplished, and driven.

Her father held a high-profile government position as a U.S. Ambassador. I read that her parents were strict and conservative.

Her mother didn't allow her to wear make-up and had Suzanne wear long skirts on the school bus.

What her parents might not have known is that apparently Suzanne would change out of those clothes and accessorize herself before entering school—this according to friends.

Suzanne's friends and family loved her immensely. Who wouldn't? She was exceptional. She was focused. She was fun and loving. She had ambition. She was committed to her physical fitness and was strong of both mind and body.

At the time of her death, Suzanne was engaged to be married to a handsome Marine. She was also graduating from Marine aviation school that day. Life was looking very good, everything was in place, and wonderful adventures awaited her.

Unfortunately, she might have made some poor choices in men. At 19 years old, many of us aren't experienced enough in life and love to make all the right choices. We don't often make all the right choices throughout much of our lives for that matter.

A young woman could easily fall prey to the charms of a handsome ladies' man who was just a bit older and more experienced than she was. Then again, even experienced women can fall prey to the charms of bad men.

Serial killer Ted Bundy was handsome, intelligent, and supposedly very charming. This may explain how he was able to gain the trust of so many female victims: luring them with a sense of safety and normalcy into his death trap.

Of course, we remain unaware of the deep emotional perversions that reside beneath the surface of people we don't know well enough until we, in fact, do know them well enough.

Nashville Scene newspaper writer William Dean Hinton

penned this account:

> "In the early morning of July 12, 1985, a woman's nude body was discovered feet-first against a tree in a city park in Millington, Tenn., a town of 10,000 residents about 20 minutes north of Memphis. Her face was bruised and beaten, her hair matted with blood, strangulation marks visible around her neck. A 31-inch stick, taken from the tree above, had been shoved so far into her vagina, twice, that it punctured a lung. In all, there were more than 100 individual injuries to Suzanne Collins' body. Her murder is still regarded as one of the most senseless and gruesome homicides in Shelby County history. To this day, no clear motive can explain why it happened." [15]

Suzanne had endured over 100 injuries while still alive, including a fractured skull and a tree branch shoved inside her repeatedly so far that it pierced her lung.

The medical examiner opined she could not have lived more than 15 minutes after the second penetration of the branch. I reviewed the autopsy photos of this victim. What animal did this? Someone hated her or hated him or herself. I forced myself to study the pictures repeatedly for clues.

I investigated this case 13 years ago, and the autopsy photos still flash in my mind, much more frequently than I would ever have imagined. Honestly, as much as it saddens me to be reminded of those horrific images, part of me is okay with it because I feel it keeps Suzanne's ordeal, and thus all victims, relevant for me. While defending citizens accused of violent crimes, I would never want to lose empathy for the victims.

At the time of Suzanne's murder in 1985, Sedley Alley was depressed and using drugs and alcohol regularly. He missed his children terribly. They were back in Kentucky, living with his parents after his wife's death. Because he was a mess, his parents sought custody. The kids would have rather lived with Sedley, even after he eventually remarried, but their grandma hated Sedley's new wife.

Alley's daughter April told me wonderful stories about her father. Sedley never raised a hand to them. He was authoritative and firm, yet soft spoken. Sedley wrote their mother poetry. He played giddy-up with both of them on his knees, bouncing them up and down together.

April Alley told me how her father raked up a bunch of leaves from the yard and covered the hood of the car with them. He put her in the car and drove down the street with leaves flying everywhere. She had so much fun that she asked him to do it again and again. He raked the yard and did it all again, twice more.

April recalled Sedley having been a really good dad, and said she didn't witness any altercations between him and her mother growing up.

Here is an overview of the evidence presented by the State of Tennessee at Sedley Alley's 1987 trial:

- Blood on his shorts (type O, same as victim),
- Blood and hair swipes on the outside of his car (type O and brownish-blond, same as victim),
- Witnesses saw his car speeding toward the victim and heard her scream at the abduction scene,
- Witnesses further identified his car as the car at the abduction scene because of its loud muffler,
- He was identified by a witness as standing next to the

victim at the abduction scene just before her screams,
- He started his car with a screwdriver (a mechanical failure he never fixed) and a screwdriver with blood on it was found somewhat near the scene where the victim's body was found,
- A Danvers Restaurant napkin was found at the scene of the body, and three such napkins were found inside Sedley's car,
- He was drunk,
- His ex-wife died by choking in the bathtub at home without witnesses (now considered to be "under suspicious" circumstances),
- He confessed to murdering Suzanne Collins,
- He led police to the location where the body was earlier found by police.

After spending a few days in the small federal defender's office reviewing the file, as I typically do next, I went to meet Alley in person on Riverbend Maximum Security Prison's death row in Nashville, Tennessee.

Every client I have ever visited on death row is shackled to the hilt, hands and feet. The moment the guard presents them, I can tell whether they are generally cooperative or not by the way the guard treats them.

As a licensed private investigator for the defense, I'm given the same confidential accommodations in prisons as an attorney. I'm considered an extension of the attorney in this regard. This means that I meet with incarcerated clients face-to-face, in person, and not through glass. It is called a "contact visit" or a "professional visit."

We are alone. We can touch one another. It is not recorded, not surveilled, and no guard is outside our door. There is a guard stationed at the desk across the building entry room, not far from our door. If I want the guard's attention, I bang on the glass or buzz them on the intercom if there is one. The prisoner and I are in the same small room, completely alone together until I call a guard to let me out.

The first time I experienced this it was a little unnerving. But at this point, even in my young career, it was already old hat.

Procedurally, I must obtain permission from the prison warden to visit any inmate. This is accomplished via written request from the attorney. Then I sign in at the central guard station outside the prison gates and barbed wire, adjacent to the parking lot. I put all of my personal belongings in the car or a guard station locker, then get searched either by walking through a metal detector and/or by being patted down.

After the pat-down, the guards allow me to enter the connecting walkway between the guardhouse and the inmate housing units. Riverbend Maximum Security houses a handful of my clients, all of whom are on death row.

As I walk the grounds inside the barbed wire perimeter fencing of Riverbend, I can hear whistling and eager male voices directed toward me. Some are whimsically complimentary and some desperately ask me to represent them.

I guess I look like an attorney. Most folks say I hold myself like a cop. I look forward and keep moving. Sometimes I smile and say hello, but on this day I'm focused on meeting Mr. Alley and the interview ahead of me. There is no guard walking alongside me, but the inmates can't reach me anyway. Each pod or housing unit's outside yard is enclosed by additional fencing that isolates it further.

I look anxiously for Building C. Finding it, I ring the buzzer at the entry door and hear the door lock click open. While tugging the big handle I'm nearly pulled forward off my feet by the heavy weight of the solid metal door.

The moment I step inside, the door quickly closes behind me, locking itself. I wait in between the double set of doors. The purgatory of the penitentiary, I think to myself. What would happen if they forgot me here? There's no water, no bathroom, and no one can hear me locked in between thick metal doors and cement walls.

On previous visits I've had to wait in between these doors, in this three-foot-by-three-foot space, for quite a while. At least it seemed like a long time. It was probably only a couple of minutes.

When the outer door locks, the inner door opens, and I walk through it into another guard station for Building C. I sign in again, telling them who I want to see. Usually they know I'm coming and who I'm scheduled to see, but sometimes they have to radio up to the main guard station for verification. I then wait alone in a designated room.

There are two doors in this room: one door from the guard area, and another door on the opposite side of the room leading to the inmate cellblock. The door I came through was solid metal with a thick glass window framing a diamond pattern of lead wire within the glass. The door on the other side of the room is made of only thick prison bars, the same as a jail cell door, with open air between the bars. I can hear myriad inmates' voices and lots of activity on the other side of the barred door.

The room contains four attached plastic orange bleacher seats. No table. Nothing to hide behind.

Did I tell you that I'm shy? I was never comfortable engaging strangers, not to mention serial killers. But truthfully I'm fascinated to meet and interview a serial killer. I wait only a few minutes.

A guard and a very tall man in a blue and white jumpsuit appear outside the barred door in the hallway, between the inmate cellblock and me. The guard opens the heavy iron bar door.

Sedley walks into the room and stands in front of me without any shackles and says, "Hello."

The guard locks the door behind himself as he leaves the area.

Sedley Alley is the only inmate I have ever interviewed here that is not shackled hand and foot. My clients at this facility all show up in this room with a thick chain around their waists, to which their wrists are handcuffed. Another chain connects their waist chain to their ankle shackles by a chain that holds their feet shoulder-width apart so they can't run. Alley is not shackled or cuffed at all. I smile and shake his hand.

"Hey Sedley. My name is April. I'm your defense investigator."

"I know," he nodded. We sit down in seats right next to one another.

Attorneys always give clients a heads-up when I'm coming to visit.

"Why aren't you shackled?" I inquired with great curiosity.

He tells me he is "A" level, which means he's not considered threatening or high-risk. He also holds a job in the prison. In other words, he is a trusted prisoner.

I'm a little surprised, but I'm thinking it is very cool. I break the ice by asking him to educate me on the prison system and classifications, and he kindly obliges me. He has nothing better to do this day.

Alley is a very soft-spoken, polite, and gentle man, in my estimation. Throughout my two-hour interview with him, my opinion doesn't change. He explains how his confession was coerced by police at gunpoint and by threats to arrest his wife in conjunction with the murder.

He professes his innocence once again to me. And yet, even so, he seems to accept his fate after 18 years of injustice.

Having already read a previously published book characterizing Sedley Alley as a monster and a serial killer, I'm expecting to experience something entirely different during our initial meeting. I ask him a lot of questions about his personal life and his beliefs. I want to know more about him.

He talks about his kids and his second wife Layne (to whom he is no longer married), as well as his deceased former wife Debra. He speaks of all these people in a loving manner.

He goes on to describe life in prison, his prison education, and his work for pay behind bars. It's obvious that the guards like him and aren't concerned about him acting out in the prison. His only problem there is that he's been wrongly convicted.

I share my honest opinions with Sedley, as I do with every client, about the evidence against him and how guilty he appears. He nods and then shakes his head. He tells me his side of the story in detail, after which I again ask a lot more questions. No investigator had ever come to talk with him before.

He seems happy that I'm here, but he admits he's not sure what I can do at this point to help him. Alley is resigned to his fate in the death chamber. To me, his demeanor personifies utter defeat and hopelessness.

Personally, I'm now becoming confused, and keep asking myself, "How did this nice man kill anyone in any way other than an accident or in self-defense?" Suzanne's death was no accident. She was tortured.

I assure Sedley that I will do all I can to locate and thoroughly investigate all of the evidence in his case. I promise him that I will do a good job. I also let him know that his attorneys care about him and are good at their jobs. He nods again and thanks me as he raps on the door for the guard to release me back to the outside world.

As I exit the prison, I keep wondering if everyone involved has overlooked significant elements of the case . . . and Alley is telling the truth. Either he's a great deceiver, or something is truly amiss. I'm now quite interested in investigating this case. If nothing else, it will be great work experience for me. I know I'll learn a lot.

At this time, I wasn't aware of the late hour of my investigation. The fact that almost anything I found implying innocence could not be presented in court was lost on me. All of those appeals had already passed.

A more experienced investigator would have understood the meaning of federal habeas, but I was still too green. I had never learned about the legal stuff. My job was to go out and look for evidence of innocence. That's what I do. I look, I find, and I report to the attorneys.

My thoughts at this point were focused on disproving the prosecution's case. Later, I learned that only constitutional violations could now be presented in support of Mr. Alley, such as juror bias, prosecutor misconduct, judicial bias, jury tampering, and the like. Or of course someone else could confess and/or be proved to be the real killer.

Fortunately, since I had not learned this yet, I was still focused on making a case for innocence. This oversight on my part turned out to be to Sedley Alley's benefit.

Sedley Alley: Honing the Sword of Truth

When I arrived back home from the prison, Anne was there, reading in our living room. She put down her book immediately and asked me to tell her about my interview with Sedley.

Serious, complex cases like Sedley Alley's fascinate both of us, and Anne has become my sounding board. She's smart and compassionate. She wants to help me on this case, not only because it's so interesting, but also because she wants to keep me safe.

Anne knows all about me and cars. I fall asleep as soon as the car starts rolling, unless I'm behind the wheel, in which case it takes me an hour or more to start nodding out. I've fallen asleep at the wheel three times while alone in the car. My parents used to call me April "Crash" Higuera.

This works to my advantage when I fly because I'm asleep from just moments after takeoff until landing. It feels like a five-minute flight every time. Anne got so annoyed when we flew to Australia, a 22-hour flight, because I slept 18 hours of the trip and she had no one to play with. She even took a sleeping pill and still couldn't get to sleep. I didn't need a pill. I think that I can actually sleep standing up.

Anne is everybody's best friend. She's a cheerleader and supports me in everything I undertake. I feel very fortunate to be in this beautiful home in the green rolling hills of Tennessee with her.

I tell Anne how sweet Sedley was when I met him at the prison. Then I remind myself that serial killers are notoriously charming people.

"It didn't seem like he was lying," I say.

"Well, just go and do your thing. You'll find the answers and then you'll know," she cheers me on.

"Wanna drive to Millington with me tomorrow?" Millington is just outside of Memphis, a four-hour drive round trip from Nashville.

She relieves my worries. "Sure, let me clear my schedule at work." She's always ready to help me and back me up.

I had dragged Anne down to Memphis not too long ago when I investigated a capital post-conviction case in which the defendant was convicted of shooting a mother, her son, and her nephew, and burying them all alive together in a pit beneath a grave in a cemetery. I had been tasked with locating and interviewing the defendant's comrades and adversaries.

Police alleged that this prior client was a leader of a black gang in Memphis dealing drugs obtained through a Columbian connection. This was the investigation that I disliked the most, except for the California case in which the 14-year-old was raped and left to be consumed by coyotes.

Anne accompanied me on my first interview on the gang

case. It was nice having her there to back me up (or at least watch out for me), since these kinds of snakes usually have guns.

I first set out to interview a gang associate of the client, his buddy. He was my alternate suspect in the case. Maybe he'd really committed the murder. Here's how that attempted interview unfolded . . .

Anne and I pull up alongside the alternate suspect's home and sit in the Pathfinder for a minute, preparing for what lies ahead. I'm very nervous, but Anne is even more so. I'm pretty sure I know what Anne is asking herself: What the hell am I doing in this place?

We formulate what seems like a solid plan: Anne will dial 911 on her cell without hitting "send," wait in the car watching my every step, and keep the car running.

"Anne, I'm just going to walk up to the house and knock. I'm not going inside. I'll talk to whoever answers on the front porch. If for some reason, I vanish, then hit SEND."

"Okay. You're not going inside, right?"

"Right! Definitely not. If you don't see me anymore, then call 911 and drive around the corner out of sight. If anyone comes after you, keep driving!" I instructed.

"I'm not leaving you here."

"Yes, you are!" I restate very firmly. "You drive away! What the hell are you gonna do to save me? Get killed too? Keep driving! That's an order!"

"Uh-huh."

"Don't worry. I'm not going inside. I'll be right there on that porch."

"Right. You're not going inside. Okay. Be careful honey," she cautions me.

Mentally geared up, I exit the vehicle. I walk across the street, continue up the front path to the tiny white, weather-beaten, one-story house, and knock on the door. No answer. I feel relieved, but then I realize that I'll just have to come back again. I knock much harder.

I swear I can feel lots of eyes from the neighborhood focused on the back of my head. People must be peeking out of their curtains on this tiny block. No one's outside. The air is still, the same way it was in South Central Los Angeles just before the young black man brushed up against me with a pistol in his hand. It's not a stagnating stillness, but an energized one, like the calm before the storm when all the atoms start increasing their vibration, bouncing off on another, creating static in the air. I sense the buildup of heightened awareness in my veins. The back of my wrists are prickly with adrenalin.

My anxious hypersensitivity is broken by the middle-aged black woman who abruptly answers the door. She listens to my spiel about being a private investigator who wants to speak with her son because he might be able to provide some information concerning my client.

Sometimes it's really hard to get anyone in this situation to talk. They can't believe I'm not going to involve them in a murder case or frame their child. Like really? Yes, of course, I'm getting you involved.

"C'mon in honey," the nice lady invites me in.

I'm way too polite sometimes. I smile with relief and walk into her house, focused on the interview. Suddenly I'm not thinking about poor Anne, who must be freaking out as I disappear into the house. From Anne's vantage point, she can't see who answered the door. She can only see me vanish from the stoop into the dilapidated wooden abyss.

I sit at the family's kitchen table, holding a glass of tap water and talking to the witness's mother. It doesn't occur to me for several minutes that I've abandoned Anne without any sign that I'm okay. I should've waved to her or something. Oops!

To prepare for interviews I have to psyche myself up. I enter a mental zone, laser-focused with tunnel vision. Fearless.

The lady tells me that her son is indeed the person I'm looking for, but he isn't home.

"Would you like some cookies?" she asks.

I graciously decline. She asks me what the case is about and why her son is of interest to me. I don't answer any of that directly, but only say that I hope he can help me sort some stuff out, since my client is a friend of his.

I tell her I'll come back another time and thank her for her hospitality. I stand up, push my chair back neatly under the table, and head back to the front door. Anne has probably called 911 by now.

The lady walks me to the door and bids me a kind farewell, asking if I want to take a cookie with me. This reminds me of the Shakir case. In the middle of gangland, where the kids are murdering each other, the mothers are so sweet, open, and welcoming—so motherly. There goes my argument on parenting being the cause of criminality.

Maybe it's the absent father syndrome. I remember writing a formal paper in college English offering my analysis of the childhood story, Bambi. I wrote it as an exposé on the perils of a child raised without a father. I called it "Daddy Deerest." The teacher liked it a lot and encouraged me to be an author. That was a long time ago, but here I am.

As I peer around the corner of the house, there's no sign of Anne. I look again and spot her just around the corner, watching from a different angle now. I quickly walk over and opened the Pathfinder door, ready to hear it from her.

"You said you weren't going into the house!"

"Yeah, I know. I'm sorry. He wasn't home. It was just his mother. Not a problem."

She lets me have it. "Jesus, April. Seriously?! I didn't know what to do! I wasn't gonna leave you there. I was starting to panic. I almost called 911."

"Yeah, let's get outta here. It was fine. I should've waved or something to let you know it was fine."

"Yes, you should have!"

"Yeah. Sorry. I got in a zone. Let's just go." I give her a pat on the leg and we drive off.

I really don't know how she puts up with me sometimes. I wouldn't have been too comfortable going there without her, and I'm grateful for her company. I figure cooking her a nice gourmet dinner and playing songs for her on the piano will relax her.

But first, I drag her to the cemetery to check out the crime scene. We need to talk with the gravedigger and see where the victims had been buried alive in the case of the Memphis drug dealer.

Anne didn't need much convincing to help me on the

Sedley Alley case because she was already interested in it and wanted to come along. I was truly appreciative, and she turned out to be instrumental in uncovering a major defense theory in the case. Anne, in fact, helped to solve the Alley case for the defense by formulating a highly plausible theory about the abduction of Suzanne Collins.

I then did all the investigation footwork, eventually uncovering additional evidence which supported her theory of the abduction, as well as even more dramatic evidence explaining what could have unfolded during the tragic events.

To delve into the investigation, Anne and I drove two hours to Millington, which is just short of Memphis. The Navy base and U.S. Marine training center where Suzanne Collins had been enrolled and had resided were side-by-side on the same base complex. They were gated and bordered by a golf course, Navy Lake, and Edmund Orgill Park.

Convicted killer Sedley Alley and his then-wife Layne, a Navy secretary, had lived together a few blocks off base. It was 2003, and certain things had definitely changed since the death of Suzanne Collins in 1985. By 2003, access to the base was limited, with only one main gate that was manned and operated, while the others were closed off to the public.

Back in 1985 you had to have a military base sticker on your car to drive in through a gate, and I'm guessing you could borrow someone else's car and get on base, too. In hindsight it didn't appear to have been a very tightly monitored system of controlled entry. Then again, this was considered a very safe area of Tennessee.

Even with that reputation, there had been one rape just off

base during Suzanne's training on the base. In addition, someone Suzanne knew, it seemed, had been found dead at the base of a bridge under mysterious circumstances. A friend of Suzanne's told me that Suzanne thought her friend had been pushed off the bridge.

In the back of my mind, I often wondered if Suzanne's speaking out about this "accident" being a homicide made someone on the base angry enough to hurt her. One of her friends reported to me that just a few days before her death Suzanne had told her she thought she was being followed.

Through witnesses, I learned that the ratio of men to women on the base in 1985 was estimated to be five men to every one woman. In addition, some of the military women were gay, making the ratio of men to straight women even greater. Thus, one can imagine how much attention the pretty Suzanne might have received on a daily basis.

Suzanne's reputation was that of a hard-working honors student who followed orders. Some friends, however, didn't paint her as all that straight-laced. She enjoyed tanning in her bikini at the public pool, dancing, dressing somewhat provocatively, going off base now and then, and quietly dating.

Her superiors were unaware of any of this activity. In fact, only a couple of friends knew she was dating at all. Even so, everyone agreed that Suzanne was a "good girl," i.e., virginal. She told them she was waiting for her wedding night.

She exercised twice a day, rising at 4:00 a.mm to work out, go to class, and then work out again later. Very strong and fit, she focused most of her time on her studies, politely turning away from the stares and comments of ogling men. She didn't talk to strangers. Certain witnesses characterized her as having a "holier than thou" attitude, but they were probably jealous of her abilities and physical attributes.

Sometimes she would jog at night, which was not recommended. After the rape in the local area, most women jogged in pairs. Suzanne's jogging routine and route were well-known by others. Maybe she thought that would keep her safe.

Anne and I followed the route that Suzanne jogged the night she was abducted. We drove from the naval base, northbound along Attu Extension Road, alongside the golf course, past the live buffalo pens, and around the corner toward Navy Lake. I took photos of the entire route, step-by-step.

We continued on to the second crime scene where Suzanne's body was found in Edmund Orgill Park, only a couple of miles away. Again, I photographed the scene, views of the scene from the pavilion, and camping areas surrounding the scene. Then we returned to the abduction location and started re-enacting the events as laid out by the witnesses.

Suzanne left her barracks around 10:30 p.m. to jog. She was alone. No one else joined her because they were busy cleaning the barracks for morning inspection. The next day was graduation day.

The staff sergeant had assigned Suzanne to 24-hour duty babysitting the barracks on her final day, which meant she didn't have to clean, but she was also stuck there. Suzanne took her allotted time off for physical training (PT), and went for her last jog on the base before graduation.

Two Marines, Michael and Mark, who were jogging together, reported seeing a female jogging alone toward them on Attu Extension Road. They were jogging northbound against traffic in the vicinity of the live buffalo pens, and Suzanne was jogging southbound with traffic before crossing to the other side of the road toward the pens as she spotted the two men. She was wearing a red T-shirt and red shorts and heading back toward the base. This was Marine attire, but they did not report her as being a Marine. Suzanne was less than a mile from the barracks.

She had only been gone half an hour at this point. The two Marines stated that when the woman saw them approaching, she crossed to the other side of the road, presumably to avoid any interaction with them.

The men continued jogging north around the corner. They immediately noticed a vehicle parked on the side of the road. The vehicle's headlights came on and the driver sped toward them, swerving, traveling southbound in the direction of the female jogger. The Marines described the vehicle as a brown-on-brown, wood-paneled late model station wagon, perhaps a Ford, with a ragged-sounding muffler.

The next witness on scene was U.S. Navy man Scott, who drove his white truck on Attu Extension Road off base in the same direction the Marines were jogging.

As Scott approached the live buffalo pens on the right side of the road, he noticed a female stretching on the left side of the road. Apparently, Suzanne had crossed back over once the Marines had gone around the corner. Walking southward from the buffalo pens was a man—medium build, dark tan, black shorts, short dark hair, about 5′8″. A dark wood-paneled station wagon was parked by the buffalo pens. Scott continued driving northbound around the corner in the direction of the two

Marines and onward past them.

Moments later, Marines Michael and Mark heard a female scream, "Don't touch me! Get away from me!" They stopped, turned, and darted back in her direction. When they turned the corner, they saw the station wagon on the side of the road near the buffalo pens.

The driver then sped away from the scene toward the base, carrying off the screams of a woman's voice inside it. The two Marines hauled ass, running just under a mile to the base gate to report the situation to the gate guard at about 11:15 p.m.

The guard called in the report to naval police on base. He later remembered letting a brown station wagon with brown wood paneling leave through the gate. A man and a woman sat close and quietly in the front seat, as if the woman was on the man's shoulder.

The driver exited the base and turned left. The guard did not stop the car and he could not offer details of the occupants. The Marines continued on to the base military police and gave a formal statement, as did the gate guard over the radio.

Naval police assumed there was a domestic situation at hand and put out a BOL ("Be On Lookout") for the subject station wagon. At 12:10 a.m., police stopped Sedley Alley in the area as he drove a 1972 green wood-paneled Mercury station wagon.

It was obvious to police that Sedley had been drinking. He was also sweating a lot around the neckline of his red T-shirt, and his blue jean shorts were wet. Police took him to the base for questioning. Sedley told the military police that he was on his way home from buying and drinking some beer. They didn't buy his story.

I'm not sure why, but they thought he and his wife might have had a dispute. Believing that Sedley had thrown his screaming wife into his station wagon by the buffalo pens, naval police called Sedley's wife Layne to the station and questioned her.

She explained that she had been out with friends and had not had any arguments with her husband. Both she and Sedley said they were not the persons seen by the witnesses, and that they had no disputes that night.

Witness Scott was at the base headquarters as well, and although he saw Sedley Alley at the station, he did not identify him as the man he had just seen near the buffalo pens.

Michael and Mark, who were also still at the naval police station while Alley and his wife were being questioned, were never asked to identify Sedley, only his car. They were taken out to the well-lit parking lot while Alley was inside being questioned. They inspected the car and confirmed that it looked like the station wagon they saw, but they weren't certain.

As the Marines walked away from the parking lot, Alley—who was unknown to them—walked outside, started up his car, and drove off. After hearing the noise from Alley's exhaust, the Marines now "knew" that the car they saw and heard at the abduction scene was Alley's car. Apparently, the exhaust system's sound was somehow distinctive.

Now the naval police definitely did not believe the Alleys, and they surveilled their house for the rest of the night, logging the times at which they saw Sedley out on his front porch. Police logs indicated that Sedley did not leave his house for the rest of the night.

What was the most obvious misstep made in this case? It was a two-part issue.

First, the two Marines did not identify Suzanne as a fellow Marine even though she was wearing a red U.S. Marines T-shirt and shorts. Sedley Alley's wife wasn't a Marine and was not wearing red attire.

Secondly, instead of simply concluding that Sedley was some drunkard beating up on his wife, why didn't the military police check the female barracks to see if anyone was missing? Not only did they fail to undertake this search, but they canceled the Be On Lookout alert and discontinued any further investigation, except for watching the Alley house for the rest of the night.

Talk about dropping the ball.

When the Alleys were being interviewed separately, the two Marines were taken to look at Sedley's wife and they both said that she was not the woman who had been abducted. Sedley Alley's car was green, and the reported car was brown. Right then and there, police should have kept looking for a female jogger! But instead, Naval Investigator Rogers cancelled the BOL alert at 1:28 a.m. because he believed that Alley fit the eyewitness's physical description of the man at the abduction scene, and he believed Alley's wife was the woman the Marines saw jogging and heard screaming.

I do not consider the description, "5 feet 8 inches, short dark hair, dark tan, and black shorts" to be anything close to a description of Sedley Alley: 6'4", brownish-blond, glasses, facial hair, pale complexion, and wearing red T-shirt and blue jean shorts.

The gate guard initially reported a brown station wagon exiting the gate with a man and a woman inside. (Alley's car was green.) He later reported that the license plate was blue and white—presumably Kentucky, the same as Alley's. Was this addition to the gate guard's statement made after Alley was questioned?

At 4:50 a.m. the next morning, Suzanne didn't show up at morning muster. At 5:15 a.m. Suzanne was reported missing.

Why wasn't she reported missing at any time during the night? The police reported that no one noticed she was gone. Meanwhile she was the Duty NCO/babysitter of the barracks that night.

At 5:30 a.m. the Be On Lookout was reinstated for a brown-over-brown wood-paneled Ford station wagon (as originally reported). Why were they looking for yet another station wagon? They knew where Sedley Alley was. I guess someone decided to believe Sedley and his wife. But it was too late.

At six o'clock in the morning, Shelby County Sheriff requested that the naval police put a helicopter in the air over Edmund Orgill Park. Again, why? Because they had received information that a wood-paneled station wagon had been seen in that area the night before, and that someone had heard a woman scream. However they didn't initiate a search at that time.

At 6:53 in the morning police discovered Suzanne's dead body in Edmund Orgill Park. She had obviously been extensively tortured.

The authorities arrested Sedley Alley at 7:04 a.m. at his

home. He was still hung over from an evening of heavy drinking. The authorities took him to the naval police station, arriving at 7:08 a.m., and questioned him intensely for a long period of time until he gave a full confession at 7:23 p.m.—more than 12 hours later.

After confessing, Alley took police out to the scene where they had found the body that morning.

Alley's wife drove the station wagon to work that day and parked in front of her office on the military base. Naval investigators located the vehicle, then reported that there was blood on the outside of Alley's car.

The lead naval investigator, who had determined that Alley and his wife were lying and cancelled the Be On Lookout, issued a lengthy report. The naval investigator detailed the events starting at the time at which the Marines reported a kidnapping up to the time of the discovery of Suzanne's body, after which he handed over the investigation to local police and the local FBI.

When the authorities turned over the report to Sedley Alley's defense team, it had been redacted, meaning all of the witness's names had been blacked out. Some police departments do this, but I have never seen them also redact the name and signature of the report writer! Therefore the defense was not allowed to know the identity of the investigator who wrote the report, who was later determined to be NIS Rogers.

The police must be held accountable for their writings as well as their actions. Why all the secrecy up front? In addition, why did they redact the names of the witnesses? The accused has a right to confront his accusers and cross-examine witnesses.

This is how the police deliver documents to defense attorneys.

Their argument was that they were protecting the witnesses from the defendant. But remember: the defendant is innocent until proven guilty. And keep in mind that the attorneys, not the defendant, receive the reports. How can the defendant properly defend himself if he can't interview the persons who have accused him? Is this fair?

As part of our investigative footwork, as it were, Anne decides to jog Suzanne's route and have me time her and measure the distance. This is a great idea. We also measure the route of the two Marines, Michael and Mark, in relation to Suzanne's route, taking into account each of the witness's testimony. In effect, we re-enact the incident according to three eyewitness statements.

The first witness observation was that the two Marines passed Suzanne on Attu Extension Road just after the buffalo pen enclosures. Moments later they saw the headlights of an oncoming station wagon speeding by them and traveling toward Suzanne. They continued jogging around the corner toward Navy Lake.

Anne starts jogging the Marines' route from a spot just past the buffalo pens where they said they crossed paths with Suzanne. Anne continues around the corner to the point where the Marines reported hearing a woman scream—approximately 300 yards from where they had passed Suzanne to the point from where they heard her scream.

At the time of this re-enactment, Anne is a competitive long-distance runner. It takes her a little over two minutes to jog from where the Marines first saw Suzanne to the point where they reportedly heard her scream.

Recall that the Marines almost immediately saw the station wagon coming toward them just after they had passed Suzanne.

Scott, driving his white car, then passed Suzanne stretching across the street from the buffalo pens next to a man described as 5′8″, short dark hair, very tan, black shorts, standing next to a parked station wagon.

Scott's observations occurred in between the time the Marines first jogged past Suzanne and when they heard her scream. According to our measurements, Anne and I calculate this to have been a two-minute period.

It takes another minute for Anne to run back to the place where the Marines could have seen the station wagon driving off with Suzanne.

We conclude that for over two minutes, Suzanne remained standing near the buffalo pens in the vicinity of a man who was 5′8″, with short brown hair, a dark tan, black shorts, and a station wagon—<u>before</u> Michael and Mark heard her screaming.

Anne exclaims, "She knew him!"

"What?" I try to catch up with the conversation.

"Suzanne knew the guy that killed her! She talked with him for over two minutes!"

"Oh my God, Anne, you're a genius! Suzanne also had to be fighting for that extra minute it took him to get her into the car!"

The Marines said that from the moment they heard the initial scream, until they ran back toward her, the woman never stopped screaming. She screamed for a whole minute. She fought the guy.

"She talked with this guy for a couple minutes and then started screaming. Why would she stretch near or stand around next to someone she doesn't know for that long in the dark?" Anne quizzes me.

"Yes! She crossed the road when she saw the two male Marines coming toward her," I say, referring to Suzanne's usual habit of avoiding strangers. "So she definitely knew this guy. You're so right!"

"Wasn't her ex-boyfriend, what's his name, 5′8″ or something, tan, short dark hair? And how tall is Sedley?" Anne asks me.

"Yes, one of her exes was that height exactly! Sedley is 6′4″, glasses, white as can be, longish blond/brown hair, and has facial hair. Maybe her ex-boyfriend Perren killed her!"

Anne and I got into the Pathfinder and headed back home to Nashville. Upon arrival, I immediately conducted another review of all the testimony and pertinent discovery regarding Suzanne's known jogging route, history with boyfriends, habits and behavior around strangers—all in addition to the forensic reports.

Anne was certain. I'm always skeptical. I played devil's advocate all evening with her, but her theory seemed absolutely right on.

During my actual investigation, the so-called evidence in this case was becoming more transparent to me. The media reported blood inside Alley's car. Forensic reports indicated <u>no</u> blood inside the car. Damn news people!

There was blood on Alley's shorts and on the outside of his car. Some of it was determined to be human blood type O—the same as the victim—and the same type as Alley's own blood. Some was determined to be animal blood.

The blood contained a brownish-blond hair, the same as the victim . . . and the same color as Alley's hair. Investigators found hair on the victim's clothing that was inconclusive.

The tire tracks and shoe imprints did not match Alley's. No such thing as reliable DNA testing existed in 1985, but it was available now. The blood, hair, skin cells, and semen collected in the case had never been tested.

I called Sedley Alley's attorneys and shared our theory that Perren had killed Suzanne.

The attorneys gave me the green light to investigate Perren at full throttle.

Sedley Alley: From Guilt to Innocence

My ten-month follow-up investigation spanned the United States and Europe. I located and interviewed the family members of Suzanne's ex-boyfriend Perren, his ex-wife, the retired Shelby County Chief of Police, and one of the two Marines. The other Marine was apparently still emotionally messed up about this case and didn't want to talk about it.

I also interviewed Sedley Alley's ex-wife and neighbors, as well as all of Suzanne's closest military friends and schoolmates, her immediate supervisor, and Perren himself. Though he declined a full interview, I also spoke with her fiancé briefly.

In addition I recovered the state medical examiner's original handwritten autopsy notes, which had never been brought to public light in over 18 years. Without exception, every single interview I conducted and each piece of evidence I uncovered either had no relevance or pointed to Sedley's innocence.

Let's first talk about forensic "science." The most reliable forensic evidence is DNA. However, even DNA testing can be fraught with human error and corruption by mishandling or contaminating evidence.

Some people believe that fingerprint analysis is a reliable science. A state law enforcement employee recently informed me that we all have the same partial prints, meaning every partial fingerprint features similar characteristics. Also, as people grow older and use their hands to work with chemicals, or handle dirt or other abrasive materials, they actually lose their fingerprints. They simply wear away.

From my experience reviewing fingerprint-analysis procedures and conclusions in cases, I have determined that fingerprint analysis is more of an art than a science. While fingerprint analysis can be valuable, in some cases, given proper analytical training, technical precision, and strict adherence to procedures, it still is not infallible.

Beniah Dandridge was exonerated and freed after spending 20 years in prison. Dandridge was convicted for murder when three examiners claimed his fingerprints matched prints found at the crime scene. In reality, the fingerprints were not his, and strong evidence suggests they actually belonged to the victim's son. [16]

Are handwriting analysis, shoe prints, tire prints, fibers, bite marks, and voice analysis irrefutable, reliable science? No. Polygraphs, i.e. lie detectors? Hell no. In fact, polygraph results are not allowed into court as evidence because they are so unreliable.

Toxicology, as we know from the Schreiner case, is limited in its usefulness in forming reliable conclusions about certain events.

Ballistics? A form of tool mark analysis,"ballistics" refers to the unique marks left on the bullet and bullet case when a bullet passes through the barrel of a gun and scrapes the unique surface characteristics of the inner barrel. Nowadays, gun parts are manufactured from molds and casts instead of being hand milled. As a result, "uniqueness can no longer be presumed." [17]

And the pattern of bloodstains does not prove how the blood got there. Like gunshot wounds, bloodstain trajectories can be calculated for an estimated point of origin, however, such analytical estimations cannot prove what happened. I admit I find bloodstain pattern analysis fascinating and helpful in some cases. Bloodstain pattern analysis, while it has value cumulatively with other evidence, is an art form when considered on its own, in my opinion.

The following description of the value of bloodstain pattern analysis seems, to me, a good one: "Though bloodstain pattern analysis (BPA) can be a subjective area of study at times and often reliant on the experience of the investigator, the idea that blood will obey certain laws of physics enables the examination of blood at an incident scene and on items of evidence to offer at least an insight into what was likely to have occurred." [18]

Dr. Robert Shaler, a forensic anthropologist who aided in the identification of bodies after the 9/11 terrorist attacks on New York City's World Trade Center, seems to align with my belief that bloodstain pattern analysis does not rise to the level of science. He stated that the interpretation of bloodstain patterns needed peer review and more data collected to determine error rates. [19]

Of course, forensic scientists and analysts have experience observing a vast number of patterns, so they offer educated guesses which are often useful in analyzing a crime scene, but not always. Sometimes, they're wrong.

When they are wrong, innocent people can end up in jail and guilty people can go free on the streets.

"No forensic method has been rigorously shown to have the capacity to consistently, and with a high degree of certainty, demonstrate a connection between evidence and a specific individual or source," wrote a committee panel at the National Academy of Sciences (NAS) in 2009. [20]

I don't believe much has changed since then, although I do believe that DNA analysis is the closest thing we have to a consistently reliable science. Even so, DNA typing has its own set of problems, primarily due to contamination and other human errors.

The article, *The False Promise of DNA Testing,* recites portions of the National Research Council's conclusions that stricter standards must be set in place throughout all forensic sciences, including DNA analysis. It cites the case of an African American teenager named Dwayne Jackson who pleaded guilty to robbery in 2003 after being presented with convincingly incriminating DNA evidence. Mr. Jackson was exonerated years later, in 2011, after Nevada police admitted that its lab had accidentally swapped Jackson's DNA with that of the actual perpetrator. [21]

And in 2012, California police arrested Lukis Anderson for murdering millionaire Raveesh Kumra, after police matched DNA from under the fingernails of the victim to Anderson. However, Anderson could not have committed the murder because he was in a hospital at the time. It turned out that the same paramedics who brought Anderson to the hospital had also responded to the murder scene—they did not clean their equipment after administering aid to Anderson, thus Anderson's DNA was transferred to the murder scene by the paramedics. [22]

Surprisingly the bite-mark expert, forensic odontologist Jerry Mitchell testified in 2012, "I no longer believe in bite-mark analysis. I don't think it should be used in court." [23]

Scientific American published an article discussing the merits of forensic analysis and concluded that forensic sciences are flawed and in need of more research. The article further states that even DNA data interpretation analysis is subjective and varies by analyst. [24]

Many cases which include forensic evidence culminate with a battle of experts at trial. That is, the government presents their analysis, then a defense expert with similar qualifications and experience—sometimes an ex-cop or ex-state laboratory director—states why the government's expert is wrong.

Most people believe strongly in forensic science until they sit as a juror and hear the testimony of opposing experts. Fiction-based television is partly to blame: it feeds the general public a steady diet of misinformation. Tens of thousands of folks are arrested and convicted because of unscientific forensic evidence and unreliable expert conclusions. And even though DNA is the "gold standard" of forensic science, sometimes even DNA testing is faulty.

As I mentioned, in Sedley Alley's case the police collected hair, semen, and blood evidence, all of which are sources of DNA.

In 1985, forensic labs could only test evidence for type and category of evidence, not for a reliable source of the evidence, meaning the donor. For instance, blood type O found on the exterior of Alley's car was said to be Suzanne's blood because she was type O. And there was said to be brownish-blond hair in the blood. It could not, however, have been proved to be her blood without DNA testing.

Sedley Alley was also blood type O, and had light brownish-blond hair. Initial law enforcement reports indicated the hair in the blood on the side of the car was light brown, maybe brown/blond—the same as Alley's. But notably the report was later changed to call it blond—more like the victim's hair.

Some of the blood on his car wasn't identified as human blood at all, and there were goose feathers stuck in one of Alley's headlights. Contrary to initial media reports, the authorities did not find blood inside Sedley's car. Of course, police decided that his car interior had been wiped down.

Did Alley supposedly wipe the car down while under police surveillance? Does it make sense to clean blood from the inside and not from the outside of one's car after committing a crime?

Also, Alley's confession included incorrect details: that he hit Suzanne with his car, and was taking her to the hospital when she became argumentative and they fought. If events did unfold that way, then there would have been blood inside the car! Why wipe it down if that is the story you are telling?

The beat cops who stopped Alley in the street didn't notice any blood on him or his car. The two Marines, while thoroughly inspecting Alley's car in a well-lit parking lot just an hour or so after the abduction, didn't notice any blood on the exterior of the station wagon. And apparently police didn't notice anything suspicious on either the interior or exterior of Alley's car at the time they questioned him at the station.

Moreover, Alley's wife didn't notice any blood, and the people at the gas station where he stopped on his way home following his police interview didn't report seeing any blood.

Alley's wife later reported that the blood showed up the following day, when investigators located the vehicle parked in front of her office on the military base. All of a sudden, blood was found on the exterior driver's side of the station wagon. Does this make sense?

Interestingly, the street patrolman who found Alley's car parked in front of his wife's workplace wrote in his report that there appeared to be several fingerprints on the dashboard, and that the dash was dusty . . . as if it hadn't been cleaned in a while. Obviously he meant to state that the car had not been wiped down.

Law enforcement crime-scene reports noted a yellow-handled screwdriver recovered from the roadway within one-half mile of the location of the victim's body. Many hardware stores sold these plastic yellow-handled screwdrivers as a standard item.

They found this significant because Alley and his wife both stated they always used a yellow-handled screwdriver to start their car. In fact, the next day Alley's wife told police that the usual yellow-handled screwdriver they used to start their car was missing from the day before, so she started the car with an orange-handled screwdriver.

The officer who recovered Alley's car parked in front of Layne's workplace the following day, however, noted a "yellow-handled screwdriver" on the front console of Alley's car.

Recall that in the Karen Anderson homicide case in which Max Roybal was charged, I interviewed the scene police officer who noted that her death did not seem suspicious. He was then called to testify on behalf of defense in Roybal's first trial.

Had I been the pre-trial defense investigator for Sedley Alley, I certainly would have presented the police officer who recovered Alley's car to Alley's attorneys as a key defense witness. If he had stated that the car had not been wiped down inside or out, and that the yellow-handled screwdriver was still inside the car, this witness could have been critical, and might have had a decisive effect on the jury's perception of Alley's innocence.

This witness might have further implied that someone planted the blood evidence on the outside of Alley's car the morning after the incident—conveniently after the victim's bloody body had been discovered.

When law enforcement officers arrested Alley, he was still wearing the same T-shirt he'd worn the night before. He told authorities that he put his other clothes in the hamper at home. The authorities used this statement to pen an affidavit for a search warrant, saying that Alley had concealed evidence.

The Navy eyewitness, Scott, who identified the man standing next to Suzanne near the buffalo pens, was at the naval base for questioning at the same time Alley was there being questioned. However, he did not identify Alley as the man he saw, nor did he identify Alley's car as the one he had observed just an hour earlier at the scene.

Apparently military police also didn't notice the multiple

blood spots on Alley's blue jean shorts, either when they stopped him or at the naval base during his questioning. No one saw any blood anywhere on the car or on Alley's shorts until the next day, after his arrest and—most notably—after both the shorts and car were in the possession of law enforcement.

There was a hair found on Suzanne's sock at the scene where her body was found. It was African-American, and most likely was picked up in the grass. None of Sedley Alley's hair was found on her.

There were tire marks and footprints found at the scene. Neither Alley's tires nor his shoes were a match.

Alley confessed, but he later reported that the officers coerced his confession at gunpoint and threatened to also arrest his wife in connection with the murder.

Prior to trial, the prosecution presented Sedley Alley's full tape-recorded interview along with a 16-page signed confession to his defense attorneys. Alley said he was questioned for approximately ten hours without the police granting his request for an attorney.

The police reports and signed confession indicated that he arrived at the police station at 7:08 a.m., and he signed his confession at 7:23 p.m.—twelve hours later. The police said they questioned him for about two hours. The tape recording of the "full" interview was just over 50 minutes in length, and included seven audible stops and starts on the recording. Naval police reported having problems with their recording equipment. Alley's confession also didn't align with the physical evidence or the injuries sustained by Ms. Collins.

Why would anyone falsely confess to murder?

Numerous scientific studies have been carried out on the psychology of false confessions—a leading cause of wrongful convictions, and public awareness is increasing as more and more DNA exonerations are reported. False confessions fall into three general categories: voluntary, internalized, and compliant.

Voluntary false confessions are a strange phenomenon. People confess to crimes they did not commit, without any influence by police, either due to guilt over something related or unrelated, in order to gain notoriety or attention of another, and myriad other psychologically or emotionally motivated reasons. Sometimes they sacrifice themselves for a loved one. Sixty people are reported to have confessed to the 1947 murder of Elizabeth Short, known as the "Black Dahlia." [25]

Internalized false confessions are made after intense suggestive police interrogation which results in the subject coming to believe that he or she actually committed the crime and simply does not remember it.

Sedley Alley would fall into the third category: compliant false confessions. This is the category that includes police coercion. A compliant confession is made in order to gain relief from a stressful situation, earn a reward, or reduce a punishment. This category seems most prevalent, at least in the media.

In 2015, former Chicago Police Commander, Jon Burge, was convicted of obstruction of justice and perjury when he lied about police torturing the accused until they falsely confessed to crimes they did not commit. "Special prosecutors had alleged that Burge led the torture of criminal suspects for two decades, coercing dozens of confessions." [26]

Retired Chicago police detective Michael Kill, who worked

under Burge, boasted that he obtained confessions in over 90 percent of murder cases in which he investigated. [27]

In the well-known Central Park Five case, five teenage boys hanging out together each confessed to raping the New York City Central Park jogger. This case was "the crime of the century" according to then-Mayor Ed Koch.

I was living and working in New York City at the time, so I knew first-hand the persistence of the media, which kept this news on the front page for a long period of time. The public's fear, outrage, and insistence that the perpetrators be castrated and hung probably contributed to police interrogation techniques that resulted in the false confessions.

The five boys were convicted and spent most of their young lives in prison before DNA exclusion—and a true confession by the actual culprit who matched the DNA—came to light some years later. There are numerous cases similar to this one that you can read about online.

At the time of Sedley Alley's trial in 1987, reliable DNA testing was not yet available. There was, however, semen found both on the body and on underwear at the scene where Suzanne was found.

The first exoneration abetted by DNA evidence occurred in 1989. Since then, well over 300 people have been freed from incarceration due to DNA tests that concluded the evidence did not match the convicted person. The Innocence Project reports that a large majority of the exonerations have occurred since the year 2000.

The Innocence Project further reports: "False confessions and incriminating statements were present in approximately 31 percent of cases [DNA exonerations]. Looking at only the homicide cases, false confessions are the leading contributing factor, contributing to 71 (63%) of the 113 homicide cases among the DNA exonerations." [28]

The National Registry of Exonerations reported that "27 exonerations in 2015 were for convictions based on false confessions, another record. More than 80% of these false confessions were in homicide cases (22/27) . . . " [29]

It is certainly within the realm of possibility that Sedley Alley made a false confession. I interviewed the Shelby County chief of police, now retired, and he admitted to me that there was something very wrong about Alley's confession. It was my impression that the police chief did not completely believe it. I could not, however, get him to officially admit he knew it was coerced.

Interestingly, the United States NIS (Naval Investigative Service) case report indicated that Sedley Alley was read his Miranda rights (Mirandized) at the scene of his arrest, then again before his confession, at which time he asked for an attorney. Then he decided to freely give a confession, then was Mirandized yet again after his confession and before taking investigators to the scene of death.

Three times? Why? Never heard of that.

Perhaps it was merely emphasis for reporting purposes. If Alley had truly made a full and accurate confession, I could forgive police for not looking into any other potential suspects. However, the fact that Alley's confession did not accurately depict the facts of the crimes should have inspired police to look deeper.

They were well aware that they had kept him in interrogation for 12 hours without an attorney. He was hung over. Did he eat? Smoke? Make a phone call? Who knows? Was the confession coerced and the details of the crime fed to him, as Alley later argued?

Regardless, there was absolutely no excuse for Alley's defense attorneys not to fully investigate the allegations on behalf of their client. That was their job! A pre-trial defense investigator could more easily have uncovered the same, if not more, evidence than Anne and I uncovered 18 years later.

Alley's wife, even after hearing that he confessed, told investigators that there was no way he had hurt the girl.

The Commercial Appeal newspaper in Memphis included an account of the murder the next day, July 13, 1985, reporting that no motive had been determined. [30]

On July 14, 1985, the newspaper article indicated that no relationship existed between Alley and the victim, and that, according to the detectives themselves, "Alley has talked very little to detectives . . . " [31] I guess 12 hours is "very little."

On July 16, 1985, the local police detectives reported being disturbed about the canceling of the Be On Lookout alert by military police. They made it clear that they did not authorize the cancellation, but that naval police did so before handing the investigation over to them.

It was further reported on this day that the authorities found blood inside Alley's car—an erroneous claim—and that authorities had not yet recovered a weapon. [32]

The prosecutor said that the screwdriver found in the road about one-half mile from the victim's body was the weapon, and that it belonged to Alley. This was also erroneous. Suzanne was killed by the repeated insertion of a tree branch between her legs. And the police further surmised that a screwdriver was used to beat her. Both the branch and the screwdriver were collected at the scene.

Most importantly, the journalist interviewed the police investigator, who was quoted as saying, "I wouldn't call it a confession. What he's telling us doesn't jibe with what's going on. He's telling us some things, but they don't add up." Without access to the newspaper's archives, I wouldn't know which investigator made this statement because all of the articles given to us by the prosecution were redacted.

Why would police black out the name of the investigator that was interviewed for a public newspaper article? Seriously? What was going on in this case?

In a Navy publication dated July 18, 1985, the military police basically admitted that their personnel made a mistake in cancelling the BOL, and that they were reviewing all the agency's operating methods to ensure this never happened again. [33]

From what I could tell, the only work the FBI did on this case was to assist local police in obtaining a confession from Alley, and assist the prosecution in profiling Alley for inclusion in trial arguments.

After he confessed, afraid for his life, Alley made up a story about hearing voices that told him to kill the young woman.

Alley's inept trial attorneys went with the lazy insanity argument without ever investigating the incident and Alley's potential innocence. They could have discovered all of the evidence that Anne and I unearthed some 18 years later.

Alley's prior appellate attorneys were no better. They presented no new evidence because they all believed Alley was guilty and insane, and that there was no innocence to discover.

Because he had confessed and no one investigated the crime on Alley's behalf, it took the jury less than three hours to convict Alley at trial. He did not take the stand in his own defense.

Sedley Alley was sentenced to death.

Sedley Alley: The Other Truth

N*ashville Scene* magazine's writer William Dean Hinton wrote: "In the early morning of July 12, 1985, a woman's nude body was discovered feet-first against a tree in a city park in Millington, Tenn., a town of 10,000 residents about 20 minutes north of Memphis. Her face was bruised and beaten, her hair matted with blood, strangulation marks visible around her neck. A 31-inch stick, taken from the tree above, had been shoved so far into her vagina, twice, that it punctured a lung. In all, there were more than 100 individual injuries to Suzanne Collins' body. Her murder is still regarded as one of the most senseless and gruesome homicides in Shelby County history. To this day, no clear motive can explain why it happened."

Does Hinton's article give you a clue? Why didn't they look for motive? Sedley Alley had no motive.

Perren was Suzanne's other boyfriend of only a few months, or—since she was then engaged to someone else—her estranged boyfriend. Did he have a motive?

Suzanne was well-known as a virgin. Whether that was true is immaterial. Perren might have been upset with Suzanne for one or more of the following reasons:

1. She would not have sex with him (purely conjecture on my part),
2. She was engaged to someone else, or
3. She was leaving the base soon for adventures in a different state without him.

Suzanne's new love was a tall, blond, and handsome Marine. In addition, Perren knew Suzanne's jogging route. He might have intercepted her to try and convince her one last time to be with him. Things might have become ugly, at which point he took his anger out on her.

The rape, torture, and murder of Suzanne Collins, to my mind, bore all of the classic signs of a crime of passion.

It was "a personal vendetta," as one of Suzanne's good friends described it to me. This close friend of Suzanne's completely supported Alley's innocence. In fact, she believed the military covered up the details of Suzanne's death. This friend wrote a letter for me to present to the court, begging the judge to approve testing of the crime scene DNA.

Suzanne was found face down, and had suffered over 100 individual injuries. She was raped, then brutalized with a tree branch. No serial killer was on the loose who used this modus operandi. Someone she knew did this. The guilty party was someone who had lost it . . . who hated something Suzanne represented in his twisted mind. This appeared to be a classic case of a rape and murder in which the victim knew her attacker.

Sedley Alley and Suzanne Collins had never met.

I asked Alley's attorneys if I could bring Anne along with me to interview Perren. Yes, in fact I was apprehensive. I didn't want to miss anything, and wanted someone else to witness his words and actions. The attorneys immediately arranged our flights.

Anne and I were nervous about the interview. I don't think I slept much on the flight. After landing, we rented a car and checked into the airport hotel. We immediately bought a drink at the bar before having dinner. I played it cool, like always. I could see that Anne was very anxious. We would set out on our journey to locate Perren in the morning.

At 10:00 a.m. Anne and I set out with our local map to locate the Perren residence. By 11:00 a.m., we find ourselves sitting outside an upscale, gated suburban community.

"Damn!" I'm pissed. "How the hell are we gonna get in there?"

We wait a little while, but no one drives in or out. We wait longer. Still no one comes or goes. Finally, I use the intercom and buzz Perren's number.

A man answers. "Yes?"

"Oh, hi. I'm looking for Mr. Perren. Do I have the right address?" I ask.

"Yes, I'm him. Who is this?"

"Oh, hi Mr. Perren. My name is April. I'm a private investigator from Tennessee, and I was hoping you could help me with some information about Suzanne Collins. The case is coming to a close, the man convicted is about to be executed, and we're just crossing some routine things off our list."

"Oh?"

"Yes, no big deal, just hoping that you may be able to shed

some light on the connection between Suzanne and her killer, Sedley Alley. It's a done deal, and like I said, we're just crossing things off our list and want to find the connection between them."

"I have to leave in about five minutes to take my daughter to softball." He's trying to get rid of us.

I need him to open the gate. Coming back at another time is a really bad idea. I don't want him to plan what he'll say to us later.

"Oh, no problem, it won't take long, if we could just talk for a few minutes. We flew down here from Nashville. Long way."

The gate opens. I'm relieved. In my state of hypersensitivity, I think I can hear Anne's heart beating out of her chest one step behind me as we walk the groomed black asphalt roadway toward his lovely residence. He meets us at the curb in front of his house.

There he is. He stands five foot eight, maybe nine inches in my estimation. That's my height, so we're standing eye to eye.

He is very tan, with short dark hair and a medium build, exactly like the man described in 1985 at the scene of the abduction. I shake his hand and introduce myself and Anne. She does not shake his hand and stands off to the side behind me.

"So, just quickly then, you and Suzanne dated, right?"

"Yes. I had just dropped her off at the base that night. She was going to change and go jogging."

"Oh, you did?" I foolishly say, startled by his truthful answer. You never know what a witness is going to tell you—a good reason to speak to all of them.

Perhaps my visible reaction fueled his awareness that he shouldn't have said that. "Actually, maybe it was in the morning that I dropped her off." He changes his story right away. "She had spent the night at my place."

Yeah, sure she did, I think to myself.

"Ah. Okay. Well, maybe that's why there was some confusion about witnesses seeing Suzanne in two different cars that day. They saw a boxy white car around her when she was abducted." I improvise, attempting to covertly encourage him into divulging the type of car he drove at that time.

"Oh, I would have driven an old Dodge Aspen station wagon."

I know for sure I hear Anne gulp loudly behind me, but I don't turn to see if she's still standing after his comment . . . or has fainted.

I casually stay on topic, "Oh, yeah those were pretty popular then, with the wood-paneling on the sides, right? My friend had one like that."

"Yeah," he chuckles. "It had dark brown paneling," he informs me.

I know if I turn around right now to look at Anne, she will be in a standing coma.

He states that he lived at Aspen Grove Apartments at the time.

Instantly, I recognize that this statement is an unconscious misstatement on his part. I know that wasn't the name of his apartment complex, but rather the model of the station wagon: Dodge Aspen. He knows he made a mistake telling me about the car. He's flustered.

"Okay, definitely not you, of course," I reassure him. "So, anyway . . . " I continue, minimizing the significance of the car, "Did Suzanne have any connection to Alley that you are aware of? Did she ever express any concerns about any men on base, or mention that anyone was bothering her?"

"No. Nothing like that," he says.

"Did you know the Marine she was engaged to, Gary?"

"Sounds familiar. Might have been someone she dated before me." He explains that he and Suzanne dated for about four months, having hit it off instantly. They were dating at the time of her death.

He smiles and tells us that she thought it was exclusive, but he had a couple of girls on the side. His parents were coming to meet her the day she was killed. He recalls things he and Suzanne talked about, how his grandparents loved her, and how he still thinks about "it" (her murder) from time to time.

"I hope they have the right guy," he says inquisitively.

"Indeed, we hope so." I'm thinking his comment is strange. No one said they did not have the right guy.

"Didn't he also kill his wife?" he asks me.

"Well, he was never charged with her death, so I don't know," I respond.

Perren apologizes for not being more helpful, and ends our brief yet substantial conversation by telling me that the police questioned him during the initial investigation.

I shake his hand and thank him again, handing him my business card with my cellphone number in case he remembers anything else. I apologize for bothering him on a Sunday morning. (Sundays are my favorite days to find witnesses at home, so that's when I usually schedule cold calls.)

Perren turns, picks up the newspaper thrown onto the end of his driveway, and saunters like a bloody-mouthed rat digesting roadkill on his way up into his garage.

Anne and I walk back to the rental car.

"I almost asked him if I could use his bathroom, that bastard!" she says, all revved up.

"Why? You have to go right now?" I ask naively.

"I just wanted to get hair from his hair brush, steal his toothbrush, or something so we could compare it to the DNA at the scene." Anne is furious. She says the hair stood up on the back of her neck when we first saw Perren. Mine too.

"Yeah, his statements were creepy." I say.

We find a place for lunch and then head straight to the airport. We both want to get out of this town. Our flight doesn't leave until evening. We're both drained and stunned at Perren's self-incriminating comments.

"I wonder what he's doing right now. If he really did it, he must be freaking out," I suggest to Anne.

"I would be if I were him! We better be careful and make sure he's not following us or something."

"Anne, you think he knows we suspect him of murdering her? Nah. He's not gonna draw attention to himself. Don't worry."

As soon as I hear myself say those words, I start to wonder if he would be so stupid. We're both creeped out for the rest of the day and anxiously await our flight time.

There are only a handful of travelers seated near us in the waiting area at our airport gate. Anne isn't actually sitting. She's pacing. I sit in my own row of seats, not bothering anyone. Though there are many open seats all around, a friendly middle-aged gentleman sits down next to me and immediately strikes up a conversation with me.

Anne is now sitting across from me in the row of seats facing us, listening in with great interest.

"You flying to Nashville?" he asks me.

"Yes." I'm thinking: "like, duh."

"You here on business?" he further inquires.

"Yeah, you?"

"I live here. What business are you in?"

"I'm a private investigator. How 'bout you?"

"Oh, how interesting. I'm an accountant. Doing some work in Nashville for a couple days."

"Nice. Good time of year to visit Nashville." I make small talk with him.

I notice that Anne is now glaring at me straight on, and she motions me to get up. "Have a good flight. See you in Nashville." I said as I dismiss the nice man.

"Are you crazy?!" Anne chastises me as we walk out of the gate area.

"Why?"

"That guy could be working for Perren! Did you notice he has no luggage?" she educates me.

"C'mon Anne, you're losing it. We don't have luggage either. Relax. People talk to me all the time in airports. I'm just being friendly. Our plane is here. Let's go."

Anne watches over my shoulder the entire time we're boarding the plane, like a scared gopher popping up and down from a safe hole in the ground.

"See, he didn't even get on the plane!" she exclaims with increasing intensity.

"He didn't? Are you sure?"

"Yes, I'm sure!"

I take a quick gander around the plane ever so nonchalantly. She's right. I don't see the accountant.

"Get up to use the bathroom and take a look," I command Anne.

"No! He's not on the plane!"

Okay, now she's making me nervous.

"For all we know," she suggests "he was following us all day after we went to Perren's."

"Seriously? You really need to calm down. He's not following us. What's he gonna do anyway? Follow us home and kill us?" I didn't even like hearing myself say these words. Anne has a way of making me crazy. She gets a little emotionally heated at times, especially when she's sure of something and it's a matter of importance to her, like politics.

"He did not get on the plane. He was just making sure we left town," she states.

"Okay, then good. We left and he's not following us anymore." I try to calm her down.

We land in Nashville a few hours later. You know me, once I'm in a moving vehicle, I'm out. I imagine Anne's eyes were wide open and continuously scanning the plane from her seat throughout the entire trip.

Since we have no luggage, we're able to walk quickly through the airport to our car. Anne continues to look around us intently the entire time. She's especially nervous in the parking lot. We locate the car and exit the airport without incident.

"Okay, satisfied? Now please relax, you're freaking me out!" I beg her.

We make the 45-minute drive home without anyone broadsiding our vehicle or shooting at us along the way. It's late and dark outside. The beautiful country moon is the only thing following us home—in my estimation. We drive up our long private, wooded driveway winding to the back entrance of the darkened house situated in the hills of Tennessee.

Our four beautiful, big, happy dogs trigger the sensor light and greet us at the fence gate with welcoming smiles and wagging tails. It's a relief to be home, and a relief that no one hurt the dogs as a warning to us to shut up.

The house is large, with five bedrooms, a great room, kitchen, dining room and porch. Anne turns on all the lights. I follow her and we open all the doors, including the closets, before we finally relax and drink some wine. I sit at my desk and type up my notes from our interview with Perren.

On this night neither of us is feeling comfortable living alone in the woods. We're both still on edge from the events of the day.

During the week Anne remains stressed. Every time we return home, we search the entire house. After a few more days we both calm down.

Anne and I had recently bought a second home in South Lake Tahoe, and I got a little side job doing home renovations with a friend there. I was helping with painting, tiling, and carpentry work. Home renovation is another true passion of mine.

The attorneys filed my affidavit with the court in which I indicate what my investigation has uncovered about Perren, including that he matches the eyewitness description of the man at the abduction scene, knew Suzanne's jogging route, admitted he was with her the night she was killed, and more. My statements were now official public record: anyone could read them . . . including Perren!

Anne wasn't happy about this publicity, and it put us both back on high alert. Since I handed Perren my phone number, I wondered if he would read about the affidavit and call me.

I flew off to Tahoe for a couple of weeks as planned, looking forward to some renovation projects and beautiful scenery. I was still concerned for Anne's well-being, so I asked our handyman, Jerry, to check on her daily. I called her often as well.

It seemed as though everything was back to normal. Or was this the calm before the storm? I made my daily call to Anne after work on Thursday, but couldn't reach her.

At approximately 6:30 p.m. Nashville time, she still wasn't answering her phone. She should have been home from work by then. Surely she would have called me if she'd had a change of plans.

Seven o'clock came and went, and still no answer. Maybe she went out with friends. At 7:30 still nothing. I started to panic. I called Jerry. He knew all about Perren. We'd already asked him to be on guard.

"Have you seen Anne today Jerry?"

"No. I haven't been over there. Is there a problem?"

"She's not answering her phone. Can you go over and check on her please?" I requested.

"Yeah, sure." Jerry was very protective of Anne, me, and the dogs. He had known Anne and her family for many years.

Twenty minutes later, Jerry called me in a very excited state.

"April! Anne isn't here! Her car is here and her purse is on the table. April, get this, her house keys are inside her purse! I looked all through the house, even in the closets and under the beds thinking the worst mighta happened, but she's not here! I can't find her!"

"What?! Are you sure? Maybe she's out jogging. Are the dogs okay?"

"Yeah, they're all fine. I checked everywhere. She's not here!! Should I call the sheriff?"

"Jesus Christ. Jerry, go down to the creek and look around."

"Yeah, okay, didn't do that."

Click.

Five minutes later, Jerry called out of breath. "April, she's not there either. Should I call the sheriff?"

"Maybe you could drive through town and see if you see her," I urged him.

"April, her purse is on the table and her car is here!"

"Just take a quick drive through town please. If you don't see her, drive to the sheriff." (The town is a mere four or so blocks long.)

"Right. Okay. Bye!"

Click.

I was actually concerned at this point that something had

happened. Perhaps Perren wasn't involved, but something was amiss. Twenty minutes later, my cell rang again from an unknown number.

"Hello?"

"Honey, it's Anne."

"Where are you? Are you okay?"

"Yes. I'm sorry I didn't call you. Nancy came over and we just went out to listen to some live music in town. There's a singer she likes performing here tonight. I was pretty surprised to see Jerry walk into the place looking for me."

"Yeah, well, I thought, you know, Perren may have gotten you."

"I know. I'm still worried about that too. I'm fine. I'm heading home now. Thanks for worrying. I'll call you in a little bit."

This was some Karmic response to my insensitivity while Anne waited for me in the car during my Memphis gang case interview—when I disappeared into the house without a sign to her. Payback.

I wondered if my paranoia and emotions were typical of female investigators. Do guys go through this? Cops? Probably not. I "see" so much violence on a daily basis in my casework that the fear creeps in sometimes. Anne's paranoia fueled mine, and I'm overly-protective to begin with.

I emailed my mother and described Perren to her, explaining the situation. I instructed her not to answer the door to any unknown persons. She said she'd be attentive.

Living in the countryside without close neighbors has always been both freeing and a bit scary to me. No one can hear you scream. To make matters worse, the daughter of the family that lived in our house many years ago had put a shotgun in her mouth and killed herself in one of our bedrooms. We only used that room for storage.

This case made me realize I have some residual cell memory around home invasions since childhood. When I was about 11 years old, our home was burglarized. The intruder(s) slashed the furniture, emptied all the drawers, killed my pet turtles, and poisoned our family cat. That was very traumatic for a kid.

Honestly, I think Anne had a lot to do with the emotion around this Perren situation. Generally speaking, I'm pretty stoic when left to my own devices. But if someone you love is scared, it definitely heightens your own senses.

Anyway, I refused to let any crazy little fears get in the way of my work on Sedley's behalf.

Before meeting Perren, I interviewed his family members and his ex, who all unwittingly told me potentially incriminating things relating to him. He often drove a brown wood-paneled station wagon, and rigged his cars with loud mufflers and big tires.

He was very taken with Suzanne, according to his family, and was still getting over his Suzanne-look-alike ex at the time of Suzanne's death. Perren himself told me he had just dropped Suzanne off at the base that night, and that he often jogged with her. He also told me he believed he was Suzanne's exclusive boyfriend at the time of her death.

Did he find out about her fiancé? Did he find out that she'd made plans of her own to move out of state and be with her fiancé in California? How surprised, and perhaps angry, was he to find out that Suzanne was seeing someone else? Why would he still tell me she was exclusive with him when she was, in fact, engaged?

Perren appeared quite normal: like an upper middle class soccer dad. Did he block it all out? Was he trying to throw me off his scent, acting as if he had no reason to be angry with Suzanne? Or is this all merely coincidence?

Suzanne's fiancé assumed that he and she were exclusive as well, which was more likely. Perren said Suzanne spent the night with him the day prior to her murder, yet her friends told me she was a virgin and would never stay overnight. To my mind, Perren was clearly off.

Can you imagine a man so tormented by having lost the prior woman in his life, and/or that his new flame was in love with someone else, that he lost it in a truly demented way? Perhaps he had an out-of-body experience, disassociated from the events emotionally, then subconsciously created a fantasy that all was well, and still believes it to this day?

According to a prosecution expert, Suzanne's killer took the time to sharpen the tree branch before brutalizing her with it. I wondered what magnitude of force had to be applied in order to pierce her lung from between her legs. A sharpened point would certainly facilitate the effort. Who would think to do this during a random killing?

After visiting Perren's college and asking to see his records, I learned that Perren had studied outdoor survival skills.

Suzanne was athletic, strong, and trained in self-defense. Every witness I spoke with was adamant that she would have seriously hurt the guy who grabbed her, even a man who was 6′4″. The woman must have been brutalized during a significant period of time to have sustained over 100 separate injuries while alive. She screamed for over a minute before she was forced into the station wagon that took her away. Certainly she fought her attacker.

Sedley Alley had NO (zero, none, nil) scratches or bruises anywhere on his body.

Another question: how did Sedley lead police to the death scene? As described to me, during his interrogation, the police radio was on, and police allowed him to hear details about the location and evidence. They described the scene and asked him to tell them if they were right. They described her injuries and asked him what he did to cause them.

Then they put him in the back of their cruiser, lying down hung over, drove him to the location, then said, "This is the place, right?"

They threatened to shoot him if he did not confess. They threatened to arrest his wife in connection with the murder if he did not confess. I can't say with certainty whether this happened the way Sedley Alley described it, but keep in mind the mysteriously brief tape recording—featuring seven distinct starts and stops. Also note the fact that the details Alley confessed to were inaccurate.

After ten months of my investigation, we were more convinced than ever that Perren fit the profile of the killer, not Alley. I had traveled across the country and even to Italy, taking time out from a Tuscan vacation to drive to interview a close associate of Suzanne's in Verona. I was committed to seeking out allies in our effort to test the DNA.

Suzanne's own friends signed declarations and wrote letters to the court asking to test the DNA. I wanted so badly to talk to Suzanne's family, but was told that would not be appropriate. Surely, if I could convince them to test the DNA, then we would all know for certain whether Sedley committed the crimes or not.

At that point, to me, it wasn't even about Sedley, it was about Suzanne and punishing her real killer. I truly believed that Sedley could be innocent. If so, we needed to put the guilty person away.

If Sedley's DNA was present, I knew I would be fine with that result. The right guy had then been in jail since day one. Excellent!

What if his DNA was not present? The semen did not need to be his. She could have been with another man earlier in the evening. Sedley, while he confessed to killing the girl, always swore he did not rape her. If he had used that tree branch, then plenty of his skin cells, thus DNA, would have been on it.

Then again, whoever killed Suzanne also could have raped her. So whose DNA was on her and on her underwear? Whose skin cells were on the branch? Whose hair was on her body? Whose sweat? Whose blood? We had to test the DNA evidence. Why not?!

Let's say Suzanne did have sex with Perren the night before, as Perren had alluded—or on the day of, as he spontaneously stated at first. Then imagine she didn't take a shower and went for a jog that night. The semen found on her body could be Perren's from a consensual event.

This scenario was a bit far-fetched because, according to her friends, Suzanne practiced great hygiene.

Maybe Suzanne changed her mind about waiting until her wedding night. If Alley then abducted her and injured her over 100 times, strangled her, and then used the tree branch, his skin cells, hair, sweat, and blood would have been on her. His DNA would have been under her fingernails. And certainly she would have at least left some scratches on him. However, there was NOTHING tying Alley to the victim.

Even the eyewitness statement by Scott did not describe Alley.

Why was the blood on Alley's shorts and car only observed after his arrest? Several people examined his car while the police questioned Alley at the naval base without reporting any blood on it. No one noticed any blood or injuries on Alley either. Alley drove a station wagon with Kentucky plates. Notably, Perren had also lived in a state with blue and white license plates.

We never could determine whether the station wagon Perren drove had Kentucky license plates because those records had been purged long ago. Of course, the gate guardsman could also have been mistaken about which state had issued the plates. Why did he pay attention to the plates, but did not stop the vehicle or look at the people inside? I believe he said the plates were blue and white, therefore, he concluded Kentucky was the state of origin.

One thing that bothers me in retrospect is that Suzanne's wallet and a picture of her "boyfriend" were among the items naval police gathered as evidence from her bunk area. Allegedly, the photo was of Perren, not her fiancé. Why did she have a picture of him if she was engaged to Gary?

Since you may be wondering, Suzanne's fiancé had already been shipped off to an out-of-state base. Like Alley, the fiancé did not fit the physical description of the man observed at the abduction scene.

Perren told me Suzanne was dating him exclusively at the time of her murder and that Gary was perhaps a former boyfriend. Of course, police reports can be mistaken. Investigators did interview Perren and listed him in their report as Suzanne's boyfriend. Certainly Perren confirmed he was her boyfriend, and certainly police could see he matched the photo.

However, I recall that they telephoned Perren for the interview, so they would not have known whether he matched the photo, nor if he had injuries. Nor would they have observed what type of car he drove. I saw a copy of Perren's driver's license in the case discovery identifying him both visually and descriptively—he clearly matched the initial eyewitness description of the man at the abduction scene.

On the subject of Perren, the police simply noted that "the boyfriend could not provide any pertinent information."

I think the fact that her "boyfriend" could not provide pertinent information was pretty lame. That was all the report said.

A one-liner.

They never suspected anyone but Sedley, even though there was no reliable forensic evidence tying him to a two-scene violent struggle with a Marine. Is not the boyfriend the very first person police should investigate in a rape murder? Really, they just phoned him?

Preposterous.

Sedley Alley: Too Late for Justice

The Court of Criminal Appeals stated:

"Upon our review of the record before us, including the Petitioner's [Alley] motion and the State's response, we conclude that the post-conviction court properly considered all of the evidence before it. Moreover, we conclude that the record supports the post-conviction court's conclusions that the Petitioner had failed to establish that (1) a reasonable probability exists that the petitioner would not have been prosecuted or convicted if exculpatory results had been obtained through DNA analysis and (2) a reasonable probability exists that analysis of the evidence will produce DNA results which would have rendered the petitioner's verdict or sentence more favorable if the results had been available at the proceedings leading to the judgment of conviction. See Tenn. Code Ann. § § 40-30-304(1), -305(1). Accordingly, the post-conviction court did not err by denying the Petitioner's request for DNA analysis.

The District Court denied his request for testing and the 6th Circuit Court of Appeals affirmed the denial. Alley v. Key, No. 06-5552, 2006 WL 1313364 (6th Cir. May 14, 2006). Judge Boggs wrote the following in the opinion: "The compelling evidence of Alley's guilt—including his confession, his description to law enforcement authorities of his acts, and the eyewitness testimony against him — strongly suggest that he could never accurately be considered actually innocent of the crime."

In other words, the court denied our request to test the existing DNA evidence in Alley's case.

The court was not considering all the evidence, or lack thereof, but only the words of a coerced confession and an unreliable eyewitness identification: that the 6′4″, pale, Sedley Alley wearing blue jean shorts looked anything like a 5′8″ man with a dark tan, short dark hair, medium build, wearing black shorts.

Eyewitness Scott admitted by the time trial came around that he no longer remembered what the person he initially described at the abduction scene looked like. Still he identified Alley at the trial as the man he saw, without a doubt. I was told by a confidential source that Scott was paraded past Alley's cell just before his testimony at trial.

Why don't we care about the truth?

Actually, the point isn't necessarily that we don't care about the truth, because some of us do. But unfortunately, the legal system is set up to provide the convicted with a specific set of appeals and specific processes must be followed in seeking relief.

Alley's prior attorneys failed multiple times in the evolution of his case to investigate and present any actual evidence supporting his innocence, all of which could have been uncovered by an investigator before the trial.

By the time I was hired to investigate, it was already so late in the case that the judge simply did not find it worthy of further examination. Like many folks, I believe the judge did not trust the defense, or worse, he had some other agenda.

If there is proof of actual innocence, no matter when it comes up in the course of a legal process, such can always be presented to the court for consideration. The problem is, we're unable to prove anything without testing the DNA!

Alley's current attorneys, however, still had some options. It was not too late to present evidence of constitutional violations, such as prosecutorial, judicial, or juror misconduct.

Guess what I found?! Ever hear of Brady v. Maryland, 373 U.S. 83 (1963)? This is the case that gave us the terms "Brady material" and "Brady violation."

A Brady violation occurs when the prosecution withholds exculpatory evidence ("Brady material") from the defense. That is, the prosecution has evidence pointing to the defendant's innocence that it is required by law to be divulged to the defense before trial, but the prosecution does not turn the evidence over, and thus that evidence is not presented to the jury.

This serious miscarriage of justice and the ineffective assistance of Alley's trial counsel for failure to investigate sealed Sedley's fate.

It is my practice to attempt to obtain all handwritten notes and tape recordings generated by the government's (prosecution's) forensic examiners and experts. The defense has a hard time obtaining these notes in the discovery process, but sometimes the state expert turns them over to the prosecutor and the defense gets them.

More often than not, I have to visit the expert in person and ask for these notes. As you can imagine, I'm often shot down.

The notes always contain information not included in the typed, formal reports.

I drove three hours to Memphis and located the office of the medical examiner in Sedley Alley's case. Mr. Bell's notes had been stored in the state archives years prior, but his office gave me permission to have access to the materials. That was much easier than usual.

I spent half a day in downtown Memphis at the state archives sifting through multiple pages on this case via microfilm. Finally, the medical examiner's autopsy notes popped up on the film viewer. There they were: numerous pages of handwritten notes jotted down during the autopsy examination.

Somewhere toward the end of this set of notes, I noticed some handwriting up in the very top right hand corner at the edge of the page. It was a small, yet very important entry: "Time of death 1:30 - 3:30 a.m." Honestly, I had to rub my tired eyes and look more than twice at this notation. Did I read it correctly?

Wait . . . I read it again, and yet again.

Now, the Alley attorneys had a legally viable and timely cause of action—a constitutional violation of due process. Brady material! These notes were never turned over to defense before trial, nor at any other time.

Sedley Alley had been under police surveillance since 12:10 a.m., and the prosecution's own medical examiner expert, who examined the victim's body both at the scene and during autopsy, opined that she died between 1:30 and 3:30 a.m. He further opined that she would not have survived more than 15 minutes after insertion of the tree branch.

Could we legally ask for the DNA to be tested now?

The Court of Appeals continued:

"In part two of the statute the petitioner [Alley] must prove that the evidence is still in existence and is in such condition that DNA analysis can be conducted. In this case the Alley v. State, supra W2004-01204-CCA-R3-PD at page 10. 15. Petitioner is asking to test (1) the tree branch that was used to kill the victim; (2) red underwear found at the crime scene; (3) blood samples taken from the petitioner's automobile; (4) fingernail from the victim.

The State submits that the tree branch has been in the custody of the Criminal Court Clerk for twenty years. The branch was not placed in a sealed container and has been stored on a shelf in the property room. It is currently in a bin, loose, along with other evidence in the case. The possibility of contamination is so high that any result would be meaningless. The petitioner cannot show that any DNA evidence that could be obtained from the end of the branch that was protruding from the victim dates from the time of the offense.

The red underwear was found at the crime scene. There is no proof that it was connected to the murder of the victim. The victim was murdered in a public park where a large amount of trash was lying around. The underwear had no significance in the conviction of the petitioner. Because of the lack of ties to the crime itself, the underwear, even if some other person's DNA was found on it, would not exclude or make the petitioner "innocent" of the crime for which he confessed and was convicted. Any DNA results that did not contain the victim or petitioner would not have led to the petitioner not being charged or resulted in a more favorable verdict.

The blood and hair from the car was stored at the University of Tennessee at Memphis after it was tested in 1985 by technology that existed at the time that matched the victim's blood group and hair. That evidence does not exist due to a malfunction of the storage freezer in 1990.

The broken fingernail requested by the petitioner does not exist. The only reference to a broken fingernail is from the autopsy report that noted that one of the fingernails of the victim was broken. The broken piece does not exist. Furthermore, had the fingernail been found, it would have been stored with the other evidence from the medical examiner that was lost when the freezer malfunctioned in 1990."

Is it legal now to test the DNA? Yes. Will the court allow us to test it? No. This, in and of itself, is a miscarriage of justice, in my opinion. Each "side," if you will, must have the opportunity to fully examine all the physical evidence. Alley's attorneys and Alley's daughter even agreed to pay for the testing from their own pockets. Denied.

Why was the evidence not preserved correctly throughout the conclusion of such a serious case? Sure, accidents happen. Like I said, not all injustice is malicious, but simple plain error.

Alley pleaded for the DNA to be tested. He admitted to his daughter early on that he was so confused from all the evidence against him that maybe he did it and cannot remember. He definitely did not remember killing anyone.

He wanted the DNA tested to prove to himself that he, in fact, did not do it. He said if his DNA was on any of the evidence, he would accept the police's version of events and pay the penalty without further argument.

SEDLEY ALLEY: THE HOAX

In 2006, three years after our Alley casework, Anne and I were living full time in South Lake Tahoe, California. Anne travelled back and forth every three weeks or so for business meetings.

I had not worked on the Sedley Alley case in a few years now, having already done all I could on the case. In fact, I was taking a break from investigation work and just enjoying Tahoe. Alley was set to be executed in a couple months.

Then, out of the blue, I received word from Alley's attorneys that the governor of Tennessee granted a temporary stay of execution (halting the execution) long enough for a court to listen to our claims and determine if the DNA should be tested. I would be needed to testify about the Brady material I discovered, among other things. We joined the defense attorneys in hopefulness that the DNA would finally be tested and the truth be known.

Neither Alley nor I were aware that Alley's attorneys presented his kids in a video plea to the governor requesting that he please order testing of the DNA. Apparently it got Alley some traction.

A *Nashville Scene* reporter was supposed to be on board to support testing the DNA, and therefore he was granted an in-depth interview with the attorneys. Unfortunately, instead of writing an article in favor of DNA testing, the reporter turned against the defense and his article condemned Alley.

It was a kick in the stomach, and Alley was not at all happy when he learned that his kids were exposed to the public in this way. He told his daughter he would rather cease the argument and die than to put her and her brother in harm's way. There are dangerous people out there both for and against the death penalty, he told her, and they didn't need to know who she was.

To April Alley, going public was a way to help her father, who she loved dearly and missed endlessly. Even today, she continues to support DNA testing in her father's case, knowing there might be backlash from Alley "haters."

The Alley haters include Alley's own sister, who supported the persecution of her brother, and who has continued to torment his children with lies about how they grew up.

I have grown to admire April Alley very much. She has held herself together through the death of her mother when she was just four years old. She survived living with abusive grandparents, the conviction of her father when she was ten, and the aftermath of his legal battles. Her father's wisdom, especially his advice to be authentic and loving, saved her own life. She did not fall prey to hatred. She refused to play the victim, or pretend to be someone she was not.

Her father's guidance through times of her woundedness—and she is forever wounded—led her to become a strong, intelligent, accomplished woman with a lot of love and wisdom to offer the world.

April and her younger brother were objects of media attention and public scrutiny during the latter stages of their father's case. Pro-death penalty protesters hassled the children, who only wanted to visit with their Dad.

At the time Alley's attorneys asked me to testify in court, I had never done so before. This was a big fear of mine, like singing center-stage before a large audience. I was scared to death to testify.

Growing up, my parents worked long hard days and did not seem to want to hear much of anything from us kids at home. I learned to take a back seat and not to speak unless spoken to. If I chose to speak, it needed to be intelligent.

That lesson came mostly from my father. My mother liked talking with me, but she was tired from working 12-hour days. At least that's how I perceived things as an impressionable child.

Unfortunately, that fear of standing out has stayed with me far too long, deep into my adult life.

My mother was proud to learn that I would be testifying in such an important hearing on behalf of someone I believed potentially innocent. Testifying along with me would be the famous attorney, Barry Scheck (O.J. Simpson defense attorney, DNA legal expert, and co-founder of The Innocence Project), as well as a blood expert from Sacramento.

I flew into Memphis and met Scheck and the other attorneys at the hotel the evening before the hearing. We all spent a couple of hours together and prepared for our testimony. I later went to my room and watched the local news report on the Alley hearing set for the next morning and the Governor's statement relating to the DNA issue.

The next morning, I walked from the hotel to the hearing on my own. Television and news media people with microphones and cameras crowded the courthouse steps, hungrily following the breadcrumb trail of the developing story. I walked around them and went inside. No one knew who I was. They were probably waiting for Scheck to arrive.

We all converged in the waiting area inside the building, just outside the courtroom. The hearing would be covered by local television reporters with cameras inside the courtroom. No one could tell, but I was terribly nervous. I popped a couple of Dramamine—which I carry when I fly due to motion sickness—hoping they'd calm me down. They didn't help at all.

I phoned Anne to talk me down. I tried to focus on the fact that this was not at all about me, but that tactic wasn't successful either. I tried to focus on the fact that our work could save an innocent man. That helped some, but I was shaking inside my stoic exterior like a terrified raccoon trapped in a cage.

I have a good poker face, but my nerves were a wreck and my stomach was doing back flips as if my diaphragm was a trampoline.

After what seemed like a very long wait, the attorneys received word that the judge, who was the original trial judge in the Alley case, would only allow one of the three of us to testify.

What the hell was that all about? That is not justice. Please tell me why the original trial judge is the one who hears a petitioner's final plea for relief before his execution.

Everyone already knows about the reliability of DNA, so I

was hopeful that Barry Scheck, who was chosen to testify, would remember to tell the court what I had found.

Although I was relieved not to have to testify, unfortunately, Mr. Sheck was not versed in the evidence that I uncovered, and thus it was glossed over during his long and compelling recitation about the relevance and importance of testing the DNA in this case. Of course, the Court was already aware of my discoveries, through documents filed by Alley's attorneys. I sat in the back of the courtroom during Scheck's appearance. He was very passionate about his work of setting the wrongly convicted free, and believed that the DNA should certainly be tested in the Alley case, as did we all.

After Scheck finished, the judge took a recess in his chambers to consider the matter. He returned to the bench after a very long time and started by commending Barry Scheck and his Innocence Project on their fine and honorable work. I could tell Barry was not in the mood to be flattered. The judge said he was honored to be in Scheck's presence and thanked him for being in his courtroom today.

With television cameras rolling, from the bench, the judge also asked Scheck for his autograph. Unbelievable.

Then he delivered his decision: "The Petitioner's request to test DNA evidence is Denied."

More from the Court of Appeals:

"In addition, Part 4 of the act, "[t]he application for analysis is made for the purpose of demonstrating innocence and not to unreasonably delay the execution of sentence or administration of justice," also acts as a bar to testing in this case due to the history of the petitioner's claims already pursued in State and Federal

Court. At trial, in State Post-Conviction, and Federal Habeas proceedings, the petitioner has never claimed that someone else had done the crime. His attack was always as to his mental condition at the time of the offense and the failure of his counsel to successfully present his insanity claim to the jury. The petitioner filed his prior request for DNA testing less than one month prior to his last execution date. The court found that this delay violated part 4 of the statute. After two more years passed, the petitioner went to the governor, not the court, less than a week before his next scheduled execution date and attempted to get the governor to order testing. The governor granted a short reprieve so that the petitioner could file a petition in the post-conviction court to seek DNA testing. This petition was filed a week after getting the reprieve. The petitioner could have filed this petition at any time during the two years since the last denial. He decided to try to bypass the court. The actions of the petitioner violate part four of the act."

Needless to say, the court of last opportunity characterized our presentation of the newly uncovered evidence and the value of DNA testing as a "last ditch effort to save Alley only two weeks before his scheduled execution" and denied Alley's request to test the DNA.

Although I was in shock and disgusted at the moment, I'm not certain but I think I also heard that the State's request to destroy the remaining DNA evidence was "hereby granted." Or, maybe that was some sort of movie playing in my mind at this strange point. I was speechless. Now I wanted to get up there and testify!

I can only imagine the emotional response this decision caused for Sedley's loved ones. His daughter had been told a series of lies about her father over the course of many years.

April Alley was only four years old when her mother choked on her own vomit and drowned while taking a bath. Although she has no memory of it, April's close relative told her that Sedley killed her mother and that April had witnessed it. April did not witness any such thing.

She does, however, recall her father going into deep depression after the loss of his wife. She saved much of the poetry he wrote to and about his wife. April also remembers her father only ever being gentle with her mother and his kids. He never hit her mother.

The relative told April that her mother had been beaten and drowned. However, there is no evidence of abuse mentioned in police reports or on her death certificate, and there were no injuries evident during the viewing of Debra Alley in her open casket.

April was nine years old when her father was arrested for the murder of Suzanne Collins, and ten when he was convicted. The kids' own family member convinced them that Sedley caused both deaths, and maybe more, implying that he was a crazed serial killer of many women.

Schoolmates ostracized April and her brother, leaving them alone on the playground, making them feel ashamed, and telling them something was wrong with them. Their own cousin was no longer allowed to visit or play with them.

What type of people do this to innocent children of convicted parents? This is beyond cruel and beyond irrational. Support groups exist for the children of convicted parents because the shame and the untouchable label can be overwhelming.

The Alley kids effectively lost both parents in a span of five years and became emotionally and physically segregated from their peers. Their own family member lit the proverbial match beneath their feet as they were tied to the witch-hunter's stakes.

Alley lost his kids and didn't understand why until about 20 years later when April decided—for herself—that what she was hearing from others was simply not true.

As a young child, April had loved her father and felt close to him. He was her guiding light. He played with the kids, and consistently taught them to be loving people.

Believing her father was guilty, April did not visit him in prison until she was 29 years old. Alley stated in his confession that he was depressed because he missed his children. This is one part of the confession that I do believe. His kids remained in Kentucky with his parents when he and Layne moved to Tennessee for her career opportunity at the naval base just four months prior to the murder of Suzanne Collins.

Thankfully, he was reunited with his children for a couple of years before the end of his legal battles. His daughter visited him, driving from Kentucky to Nashville three times a month.

As it grew closer to Sedley Alley's scheduled execution, protesters both for and against the death penalty camped outside the prison and shouted at the kids. April recalled that as she walked into the prison for a visit, she saw a man in a car with signs on it. As she passed in front of his car, he revved up the engine as if to threaten her life for visiting a convicted killer . . . her own father.

Sedley pleaded with his kids not to attend his execution. He told April that because of all the drugs he had consumed in his life, he was sure to have a violent reaction to the lethal injection. That is what people had told him would happen. He didn't want the images of him being executed to haunt their lives.

They rejected his plea. April told me there was no way she wasn't going to stand by her father at the point where their lives would forever disconnect. She told her father she was going to be there no matter what. He resigned himself to the wishes of his two children.

Aside from the prison Chaplain who apparently cared for Sedley, I feel certain that he was comforted by his children being there with him to the end. He directed the Chaplain to hold on to the kids and not let anyone hurt them, which the Chaplain did.

Anne was in Tennessee during the execution, while I was back in Tahoe. I kept getting phone calls all through the night, back and forth, regarding efforts to stay the execution. Finally I received word about another court granting a stay. So I went to sleep thinking all was well, for the moment.

Anne texted me early in the morning and asked how I was. I said I was great, and asked when the DNA was going to be tested. "How long is the stay?" I questioned.

She told me the stay had been overturned a couple hours after it was granted, and that Alley had been executed a few hours before.

My lungs were frozen, unable to expand, and I couldn't take a breath for a few moments. Although she did not attend, Anne heard that Alley's kids both stood between the viewing audience and the glass partition through which the visitors could watch Alley be lethally injected. April Alley confirmed this account.

As Sedley Alley's children stood right in front of the glass, someone in the audience yelled, "Hey, I can't see!"

Neither of them responded, but April thought, "Good, you sick bastard. What are you doing here anyway, watching someone die?"

I'm not certain I could have held myself together hearing that while my father was being euthanized.

What the hell is wrong with people? Why would you even go to such an event, just to watch someone be murdered? Sickness abounds. The victim's family wasn't even there. Who else has a compelling reason be there, except for Alley's family and the Chaplain? This should be a solemn private family moment, not a happy public display.

Even when a prisoner is guilty, can we step back and think about his poor family? They are innocent, lost, and hurting.

Alley's last words to his kids were that he loved them and to be good people—the same message he had told them all their lives. They told their father they loved him too, and they spread their arms out wide across the glass, shielding the audience's view of the State of Tennessee's murder of their father.

Alley's final statement read:

"I cry not for myself but for those I leave behind. I am going to a much better place where I will find and know true peace. It's the ones I leave behind that I am concerned for. This world is rough and the light is dim in it. Where I am going is full of light.

This world is tough and there is a lack of compassion and love here. Where I am going there is an abundance of Love, Compassion, and Forgiveness. This world has always felt foreign to me. Where I am going is our home, our true home.

I pray that my children will find peace and be able to move on with their lives. I pray that they will find peace in knowing that my pain is through and that I am going to a much better place.

The main thing I want to say to my children, family and friends is this: Find peace and happiness, live a long life full of love, forgiveness, and hope. To my children, my family, my friends, and to those that hate and despise me, to my last breath you all will remain in my prayers and thoughts.

I hold fast to one prayerful thought, that my children, the rest of my family and friends and those that hate me will now be able to find the peace of God that passeth all understanding.

All that has been killed here is my body. A body that was worn out and tired and ready to rest. All that has happened is that my spirit has been allowed to go home and be with our Lord. To my last breath I pray for this world and forgive those I leave behind." [34]

Sedley Alley was executed on June 28, 2006, at Riverbend

Maximum Security Prison in Nashville, Tennessee. He was the second person to be executed in Tennessee in 45 years.

Sedley Alley: Stories

Many journalists and authors have written about the Sedley Alley case. To my knowledge, none of these writers have engaged in the level of investigative footwork, either pre-trial or in post-conviction, that Anne and I did. They seem more focused on creating a sensationalized, Hollywood version of the crimes against Suzanne Collins.

And while some writers did interview the Collins family for details of Suzanne's short life, they have based their accounts of the case itself on inaccurate police reports and rumor . . . as well as guessing what Alley was thinking as he (allegedly) abducted and murdered Suzanne.

While they wrote about law enforcement agents consoling the anguished family of the victim, I haven't read anything about anyone caring enough about the victim to support testing the DNA and confirming definitively they had the actual killer. If Alley is the guy, then why fear testing the DNA? It is not wasting taxpayers' money. What is wasting taxpayers' money, however, is not concluding the case once and for all to the greatest extent possible.

No prosecution or law enforcement person, that I'm aware

of, wanted the DNA tested. Why not?

To my mind, it's clear that the naval investigators blew it from the start. I'm not saying it was malicious in any way, merely incompetent. How investigators proceeded with the case after the victim's body was discovered is another story.

I do acknowledge that blind outrage can result in tunnel vision. This homicide was horrific and, understandably, the police wanted to solve it. Once a fixation on a suspect is in place, it is often hard to pry open minds and pour in common sense.

All I'm intending to point out is that anyone who writes about a subject, should, in my opinion, have firsthand experience and deep knowledge of it.

Anne had some theories about Suzanne's murder. We talked about the military having killed Suzanne. A conspiracy. We talked about Perren having killed her. And we talked about the possibility that Alley did it.

Suzanne leaves the base to jog at 10:30 p.m. The two Marines and Navy man Scott report seeing Suzanne near the buffalo pens just before 11:00 p.m., and witness the tail end of the abduction minutes later.

The Marines report the abduction at 11:15 p.m. Alley is picked up at 12:10 a.m. That gives him about an hour to incapacitate Suzanne, abduct her, drive somewhere, injure her 100 times, sharpen a branch, kill her with it, and then drive to the location at which he was stopped by police.

Alley did not have a scratch on him, nor any blood on him, immediately upon initial capture at 12:10 p.m. Did he have time to clean up? Where would he clean up? In the lake at the park?

His shorts were wet but his shirt and shoes were not. There was no water spotted in his car. There were no extra clothes in his car. It is possible he took off his shoes and washed his shorts off in the lake.

Suzanne was a bloody mess. There was no blood in Alley's car, and no forensic evidence at the scene matched Alley in any way. Later, I discovered the medical examiner's own handwriting denoting time of death being between 1:30 - 3:30 a.m., at which time Alley was at home under NIS periodic surveillance.

Is the time of death wrong? Did Suzanne die between 11:15 p.m. and midnight? That is the only window of opportunity for Sedley Alley . . . 45 minutes. But no bruises, no scratches, no cuts? There was no blood on his footwear, which was not wet, and nothing suspicious on the interior or exterior of his car upon capture. Did he kill her in bare feet? Nothing but sweat around the neckline of his T-shirt on a hot Tennessee summer night. Did he change his clothes and discard the bloody ones somewhere?

We know from the medical examiner's statements that Suzanne died in response to the final assaults with the tree branch. She might have been unconscious, but alive. I would think anyone that perpetrated this event would have injuries not only to their hands but also to their knees. Alley wore shorts . . . no injuries.

This scenario—that Sedley did all this damage in 45 minutes—while physically possible, would also have to assume that Suzanne did not fight back at all, even though we know she screamed at the abduction scene for at least a whole minute. And that Sedley Alley was brilliant enough to rush through the violent rape and murder of a physically trained Marine without leaving a hair on her body, without sustaining even a scratch. Not only that, but this scenario requires that he was so cool-headed that when stopped by police mere moments later, he showed no signs of nervousness, agitation, or defensiveness. Police reported that Alley was fully cooperative.

I cannot support the rationale to execute this man. He was eight inches taller than the man described by the eyewitness, with a different color hair, different clothes, and different facial features. He had no motive. He did not know the victim. He had no violent criminal history. It appears that he was arrested because he drove a similar vehicle with a loud muffler.

In books published prior to my writing, Sedley was accused of being a serial killer, having killed his first wife and perhaps other women. I am not aware of any evidence supporting these allegations.

To the contrary, April Alley told me that he wrote about losing the woman he loved so much. Sedley, severely distraught over his wife's death, wrote poetry about his experiences.

Reckless allegations not only affect the accused, but their families as well. April's life took a turn for the worse after Sedley's arrest on the Suzanne Collins homicide. Students at school and people in the neighborhood shunned her. April was abandoned with no immediate parents or family that supported her emotionally.

Because her brother was too young to help, April was essentially alone in her confusion. Then she had to deal with her own belief that her father was guilty—according to her own relatives and the rest of the world—the shame of his alleged acts, her own guilt for disowning him for two decades, and his eventual execution before her eyes . . . which was originally scheduled to happen on her birthday. No one thought to ask the judge to alter the date. April still wonders if the judge knew it was her birthday and didn't care.

April was the executor of her father's estate. She handed over her father's ashes to her little brother to keep. He temporarily put them in a storage pod and failed to pay the rent. She informed the storage company that the ashes were in the storage unit and that she would pay the bill, but the vendor never responded. Consequently, the ashes of her beloved father are lost forever to her.

No doubt there is much more that she has endured in her life. Most people, in my estimation, would turn to drugs or become angry, deviant, depressed, or unproductive citizens. I asked April how she managed to come through all of this so well.

Her answer: "I decided I wasn't gonna be like them," she told me. That blew me away. Wow.

She made up her mind to take care of her brother and stop listening to the lies told about her father by family members. She chose to be the person her father taught her to be. She is not certain of her father's innocence. None of us can be. Still, Sedley taught his daughter to be an authentic, loving, and productive citizen. He was her beloved role model, and because of him, she found the courage to step up in her own life.

April married a cop. She learned once again how corrupt the system can be, and divorced the cop. She is now happily married with four wonderful furry, four-legged children. April is a financial professional, owns a nice home, and plays guitar.

When I Skype with her, I see a practical, centered, honest, loving, and fearless person on my screen. She is funny. I am so impressed.

The last thing I ever dreamed working on Sedley's case is that it would bring to me such a rare find: a person of integrity. Who could ever imagine that she is the offspring of a man who many people believe was a twisted serial killer?

April's brother, while he supports this writing, chose not to come out into the limelight and face all of the skeptics once again.

April suffers from PTSD. She is still, after all these years, in therapy over the execution itself and the social repercussions of the execution of her father. She had nightmares for years.

In these terrible dreams, her father was strapped to a gurney out in a field surrounded by armed police. He called out to her for help. She answered that she couldn't help him or she'd be shot. For years whenever she was startled by revving car engines or cameras snapping pictures, she would freak out and exhibit crazy traumatic reactions. Thankfully, now she is much better.

She has nice dreams about her father, including a recurring dream that she's trapped behind a heavy metal door and her father appears in white clothes, advising her to kick through the wall. She follows his instructions and escapes. His guidance and perspectives helped set her free, and they continue to do so now.

Sedley never questioned April for not visiting him for so many years after his arrest. He understood that people were telling her all sorts of things. He never bothered her or made her feel guilty that she disowned him. He did not want to make her life more difficult than it already was. Instead, he simply welcomed her later visits.

Both Sedley and April agreed that if the DNA was tested and it was his, he should pay the price. He simply did not remember ever hurting anyone. He continued to profess his innocence and state that his confession was coerced all through the time he was executed.

When a judge sends a parent to prison, there is always more than one victim. Since our recent discussions, April has expressed an interest in helping other children of incarcerated parents lead positive lives.

It's far too easy for a child to give up, especially when they lack strong role models. The number of children whose parents are incarcerated in the United States is staggering.

April Alley is a survivor, as are Suzanne's family members.

April refuses to be called a victim. I will say that she has been victimized, not only by the legal system and its crusaders, but also by society at large. It is unjust. Yet it does offer contrast and perspective. It gave her a starting point from which to build a life on her own terms and to realize her own strength. If we are lucky, her experiences might even give her a passion and purpose to help others in similar situations.

Even so, she would rather have grown up with her father.

If we can bring awareness to law enforcement to be more conscientious, maybe some future Be On Lookout alert will not be cancelled far too soon.

If we can bring awareness that police officers sometimes arrest innocent people, then perhaps defense counsel will insist on adequate defense investigation and advocacy at trial.

If we can bring awareness that prosecutors sometimes hide

evidence to support their agendas, regardless of guilt or innocence, then maybe they will be replaced with honest ones. And maybe jurors will ask more questions, and corrupt parties will be held accountable.

Finally, judges who ask for autographs during a hearing to determine whether or not a man with viable evidence of innocence is to be executed will at least be reprimanded.

I have read commentary about Suzanne's father's ongoing sorrow and mission to feel every painful thing that comes his way without salve, asking God to retroactively lessen the pain from Suzanne's experience in that measure.

I can only imagine how disturbing it might be if Suzanne's family reads my comments on this case. I am endlessly sorry for their loss. It is unfair, undeserved, and deeply saddening.

I care about the truth. If Sedley Alley murdered someone, then he got what he deserved. If he did not, then as his last attorney stated publicly, "God help us all."

I believe the DNA should have been tested, a comprehensive defense investigation should have been performed pre-trial, and the prosecutor should not have hidden important evidence of Sedley's innocence. Why not present the whole truth? What is your opinion?

The Good Fight

My purpose in writing this book is not to criticize, but to awaken. My audience is not intended exclusively to be ordinary citizens unaware of these issues, but more importantly, the ranks of professionals who have misused their positions within the legal system.

In my own youth, my father was critical, or perhaps fearful for me. He called my dreams of being a famous singer/songwriter idealistic and naive. Now I hear myself saying that I want every professional in the justice system to be honest and work from their hearts.

I know how idealistic that sounds. But why is it so absurd to ask that we care about each other, even given our differences? Why it is idealistic to ask that we do the right thing? Where did we, as citizens of the earth, children of "God," go wrong?

Why are we so driven by greed? That's all any of this is about. Attorneys who bill hours for doing worse than nothing, prosecutors who gain wrongful convictions to pad their resumes, law enforcement who generate arrests for the sake of promotions, and judges and politicians who polish their records for re-election. All of this, in addition to influences of racial bias and other personal agendas. Sure, perhaps some of the errors of injustice are due to misinformation, but why not care enough to get it right, or to more quickly overturn it when you realize you got it wrong?

Is there a chance that we all can care less about money and ego and more about people? Can't we make a good living doing the right thing? And I thought sugar was the root of all evil. How do we sleep at night?

If Sedley Alley was innocent, then did any police, prosecutor, or judge truly protect us? Or did they make us less safe? Did they serve justice upon the guilty? Provide justice for the victim?

Max Roybal's prosecution cost taxpayers seven law enforcement agencies' investigative efforts for four years without any results, not to mention diminishing Roybal's own finances and reputation.

The same thing happened with Hope Schreiner's personal funds, reputation, and family ties. We demonstrated that there was no reliable evidence linking Max Roybal to either homicide. We later showed that Hope Schreiner had an alibi, and that Sedley Alley also had an alibi.

Why not investigate the alternate suspects in these cases: Devilia, Draggon, and Perren? Why not test the DNA in the Alley case and see what it offers? Is it a waste of money, or is the issue that the various investigators, prosecutors, and judges cannot afford to be wrong?

I am idealistic. I freely admit it. I'm a songwriter. I never intended to get into this business, but here I am.

We need more honest people defending our rights from the

greedy money machine. The more I'm involved in defending people charged with violent crimes, the more injustice and corruption I see, and the more I know I'm going to be doing this for quite a while.

I have evolved in the 15 years that I have been investigating criminal cases for the defense, yet nothing much has changed in the system, except that my eyes are open. Are yours?

I started out a believer in the justice system: I believed that cops were good, that attorneys did the right thing, that people cared, and that convicted persons were guilty. I no longer believe.

Last year, I was instrumental in saving three men I believe to be innocent from life in prison. Two men were charged with murder and one with child sexual assault.

I could write a entire book about the vast prevalence of false sexual-assault allegations, by both adults and children; it is scarily rampant and immensely serious. Every adult with an underage daughter in the house might want to consider installing surveillance cameras in every room . . . to protect the parents!

I recently reviewed a case in post-conviction in which a man was sentenced to multiple lifetimes in prison for sexually assaulting a child under the age of 14—based on no physical evidence, just her word alone.

I have investigated separate cases in which clients were charged with lewdness with a minor child, wherein the adult client is accused of touching a minor between her legs OVER her pants. A defendant faces 10 years in prison for each allegation, in the state of Nevada. How about the Brian Banks case, the Case in the News that appeared after Chapter 6? It's scary!

Ideally, we can teach children respect, family values, age-appropriate dress and conservative social media habits.

Men are going to jail based solely on the word of a child who is angry at them for being strict, or who is coerced by an angry ex-wife or girlfriend. It is truly insane and heartbreaking.

As you have read, it is beyond difficult to overturn a case, even when evidence of innocence and ineffective counsel is later uncovered.

At trial, the government must basically prove its case. In a post-conviction appeal, the convicted must prove that the government and/or their trial attorneys failed them to such great extent that if they had not failed, a different outcome would have resulted at trial.

My job is not to decide whether someone is guilty or innocent. That is the jury's job. My job is to make a case for innocence by uncovering supporting evidence and developing successful defense strategies with counsel. My job is to find evidence that creates reasonable doubt, and leave my personal feelings out of it.

The cases and events summarized in this book are real. Everything I have written about my casework is true, to the best of my knowledge, and directly from my personal experience.

Even when everyone believes someone is guilty—and they most often do when their opinion is based on police reports and prosecution theories alone—there is the potential for evidence of innocence that has not yet been brought to light. In some cases, the presumed guilty party is actually innocent.

I ask that you please care about the truth. I ask again that all practitioners in the justice system be "just." For everyone who thinks of defense attorneys and investigators as evildoers, please reconsider. You, too, could be wrongfully arrested and prosecuted. Who are you going to call for help when it is law enforcement that is against you?

As I review what I've written in preceding chapters, it becomes heartbreakingly evident that not only do we need more competent defense teams in place, but we need the courts to understand how important defense investigation is in order to maintain a just legal system and a safer world for all of us. For this reason, adequate funding for defense teams is essential.

Contemplate the hundreds of criminal cases going to trial each day, and all the indigent defendants being prosecuted. If even one of my cases involved an innocent person being convicted, or worse executed, that result likely correlates to thousands of such cases nationwide.

Please share your comments and stories by visiting the "Contact" section of my website: AprilHiguera.com.

Thank you for reading.

Now let us make our justice system work as intended.

Epilogue

Sedley Alley was executed in 2006 after 21 years in prison.

Hope Schreiner, whose neighbor dreamt that she confessed to killing her husband in the driveway, received a medical furlough in 2014—parole, in effect—and is still under supervision after eight years in prison.

Max Roybal, who was tried and acquitted for the murders of Karen Anderson and Laura Cecere, died a free man this year (2016).

Mr. Y., who shot and killed the biker in self-defense, is back in jail facing drug charges.

Mr. Z., who killed a transient squatting in his home because he thought the man pointed a gun at him, sends me texts about once every two months with a sentence or two about how beautiful the trees and mountains are and how he will love me forever.

Anne and I separated at the end of 2009 after almost nine years together. While she moved back to her hometown, I stayed in Lake Tahoe and Reno. It is peaceful and beautiful here. I love the mountains and the lake. I ride my motorcycle, hike, and cross-country ski with my good friend Julie.

I'm happily settled down for more than six years now with Virna, her (our) kids, and our four crazy Chihuahuas. Virna isn't involved much in my casework and, in fact, isn't a dramatic person at all. She doesn't spend much time on politics or watching television.

She is my anchor of calm. My rock. She keeps me grounded and keeps life simple. I need and appreciate that simple focus and rootedness in my home and in my line of work.

I still have nightmares. They used to be about natural disasters, but lately I wake up screaming the word "Devil," and Virna has to calm me down.

If you have a big heart, a strong work ethic, and a keen mind we need you in the criminal justice system. This work is not for the faint of heart, but unfortunately it is necessary. Like I said, in a perfect world there would be no need for defense investigation.

On a hopeful note:

"After a number of years in which Tennessee has seen legal twists and turns, costly confusion and probable miscarriages of justice in capital murder cases, there is a sliver of hope for improvement. A Tennessee legislative committee began reviewing work this year, after the 2006 execution of Sedley Alley was questioned because of DNA evidence that could have implicated a different person in the slaying of a 19-year-old woman; after lethal injection, one of two execution methods used by the state of Tennessee, was suspended by the governor over questions about its effectiveness, then reinstated, then suspended again pending a U.S. Supreme Court decision regarding similar concerns in Kentucky."[35]

While I present many negatives about our criminal justice system and the characters within the system, it is my philosophy that after understanding the problem, we must not dwell there, but instead put our entire focus on a solution.

It is my philosophy that in order to change something we do not want, we must put all our energy into expanding what we do want.

It is my philosophy that by empowering ourselves, we empower others.

I encourage everyone not to fight against anything, but for something; let us not fight against the dark, but for the light.

ENDNOTES

[1] The National Registry of Exonerations; University of Michigan Law School; (February 3, 2016).

[2] Redditt Hudson, "I'm a Black Ex-Cop, and This is the Real Truth About Race and Policing," Vox.com, (July 7, 2016).

[3] Betsy Brantner Smith, "Ex-cop's Absurd 'Police are Racist and Violent' Claims are Dead Wrong," PoliceOne.com News (Dec 16, 2016).

[4] Radley Balko, "U.S. Cities Pay Out Millions to Settle Police Lawsuits," *The Washington Post* (October 1, 2014).

[5] https://en.wikipedia.org/wiki/List_of_wrongful_convictions_in_the_United_States; "List of Wrongful Convictions in the United States," Wikipedia.

[6] Bob Gardinier, "Stunning 'Not Guilty'"; *Timesunion*, (June 12, 2014).

[7] Josh Levs, "Innocent Man: How Inmate Michael Morton Lost 25 Years of His Life," CNN, (December 4, 2013).

[8] Ashley Powers, "A 10-Year Nightmare Over Rape Conviction is Over," *Los Angeles Times*, (May 25, 2012).

[9] Jessica Lamb-Shapiro, "How Could She? Reflections on my Grandmother, the Murderer," *Guilt and Pleasure Magazine* (Spring, 2016).

[10] Henry Thompson, "Women Contend with a Biased Judicial System" (September 30, 2013); Plain Error; The Official Blog of The Innocence Project of Florida.

[11] Stephanie Denzel, The National Registry of Exonerations, (January 24, 2014); https://www.law.umich.edu/special/exoneration/Pages/casedetail.aspx?caseid=3652.

[12] The National Registry of Exonerations; University of Michigan Law School; (February 3, 2016).

[13] http://news.vice.com/article/why-are-there-up-to-120000-innocent-people-in-us-prisons.

[14] Wikipedia, "Rampart Scandal": https://en.wikipedia.org/wiki/Rampart_scandal.

[15] William Dean Hinton, "An Innocent Man?"; http://www.nashvillescene.com/news/article/13013208/an-innocent-man, (May 11, 2006).

[16] Carimah Townes, "Forensic Evidence Isn't As Reliable As You Might Think," *ThinkProgress* (October 21, 2015).

[17] Joan Griffin and David J. LaMagna, "Daubert Challenges To Forensic Evidence: Ballistics Next On The Firing Line," NACDL's *The Champion* (Sept/Oct 2002).

[18] "Bloodstain Pattern Analysis," The Forensics Library, http://aboutforensics.co.uk/bloodstain-pattern-analysis/.

[19] Jim Fisher, "Dueling Experts in the David Camm Murder Case: Is Blood Spatter Analysis a True Science?" Jim Fisher True Crime Blog (May 3, 2016).

[20] Kelly Service, "Reversing the Legacy of Junk Science in the Courtroom," *Science*, (March 7 2016).

[21] Matthew Shaer, "The False Promise of DNA Testing," *The Atlantic*, (June, 2016).

[22] Matthew Shaer, "The False Promise of DNA Testing," *The Atlantic*, (June, 2016).

[23] Jerry Mitchell, "Bite-mark Expert Dismisses Own Testimony," *The Clarion-Ledger.* (June 20, 2105).

[24] Michael Shermer, "How Trustworthy are DNA and Other Crime Scene Tests?" *Scientific American*, (September 1, 2015).

[25] Christopher Bray, "'Hell, Someone's Cut this Girl in Half!'" *The Daily Telegraph*, (March 6, 2006).

[26] *Chicago Tribune*; http://www.chicagotribune.com/news/ct-jon-burge-detective-accuser-seeks-justice-met-20150916-story.html, (June 1, 2015).

[27] Jason Meisner, "Burge Detective to Face Accuser Who's Seeking to Clear His Name," *Chicago Tribune*, (September 17, 2015).

[28] http://www.innocenceproject.org/free-innocent/improve-the-law/fact-sheets/dna-exonerations.

[29] The National Registry of Exonerations, Michigan School of Law; "Exonerations in 2015," (February 3, 2016).

[30] *The Commercial Appeal*, "Slaying Suspect Charged," (July 13, 1985).

[31] *The Commercial Appeal*, "No Relationship is Found Between Suspect, Victim," (July 14, 1985).

[32] *The Commercial Appeal*, "Hunt for Woman Delayed by Faulty Report," (July 16, 1985).

[33] *Navy Memphis - Bluejacket*; "Tragedy Strikes NAS Memphis"; Vol. 43 No. 29; (July 18, 1985).

[34] Memorial Service for Sedley Alley, program, (July 6, 2006).

[35] Death Penalty Information Center; http://www.deathpenaltyinfo.org/new-voices-*press-and-media.AB*

About the Author

April Higuera is the owner and principal agent of **ADH Investigations**, specializing in criminal defense investigation of violent crimes on county, state, and federal levels. April has a lengthy record of assisting wins for defense in complex criminal cases, including homicides with gang and organized crime enhancements, sexual assaults, battery, robbery, kidnapping and felony drug cases. Her work has been applauded and recommended by judges, attorneys, colleagues and clients across the country.

Currently located in Reno, Nevada, April conducts fieldwork investigations in both Nevada and California. Additionally, April provides consultation services nationally, including detailed case reviews, investigation strategies and practices, and individualized guidance leading local defense teams through their pre-trial and post-conviction investigations.

Professional contact information:

Telephone: (775) 391-4161 • Website: ADHInvestigation.com

Made in United States
North Haven, CT
05 February 2024